W9-DGH-536

THE MAN

THE CARS

THE GUITARS

BILLY F GIBBONS

ROCK + ROLL GEARHEAD

by

BILLY F GIBBONS
WITH TOM VICKERS

Photography by DAVID PERRY

MBI

BRASWELL MEMORIAL LIBRARY
727 NORTH GRACE STREET
ROCKY MOUNT, NC 27804

First published in 2005 by MBI, an imprint of MBI Publishing Company, Galtier Plaza, Suite 200, 380 Jackson Street, St. Paul, MN 55101-3885 USA

© Billy F Gibbons, 2005

All rights reserved. With the exception of quoting brief passages for the purposes of review, no part of this publication may be reproduced without prior written permission from the Publisher.

The information in this book is true and complete to the best of our knowledge. All recommendations are made without any guarantee on the part of the author or Publisher, who also disclaim any liability incurred in connection with the use of this data or specific details.

This publication has been prepared solely by MBI Publishing Company and is not approved or licensed by any other entity. We recognize that some words, model names, and designations mentioned herein are the property of the trademark holder. We use them for identification purposes only. This is not an official publication.

MBI titles are also available at discounts in bulk quantity for industrial or sales-promotional use. For details write to Special Sales Manager at MBI Publishing Company, Galtier Plaza, Suite 200, 380 Jackson Street, St. Paul, MN 55101-3885 USA.

ISBN-13: 978-0-7603-2269-7
ISBN-10: 0-7603-2269-4

Editor: Dennis Pernu
Designer: Suzi Hutsell
Associate Designer: Kou Lor

Printed in China

Be sure to visit www.billyfgibbons.com!

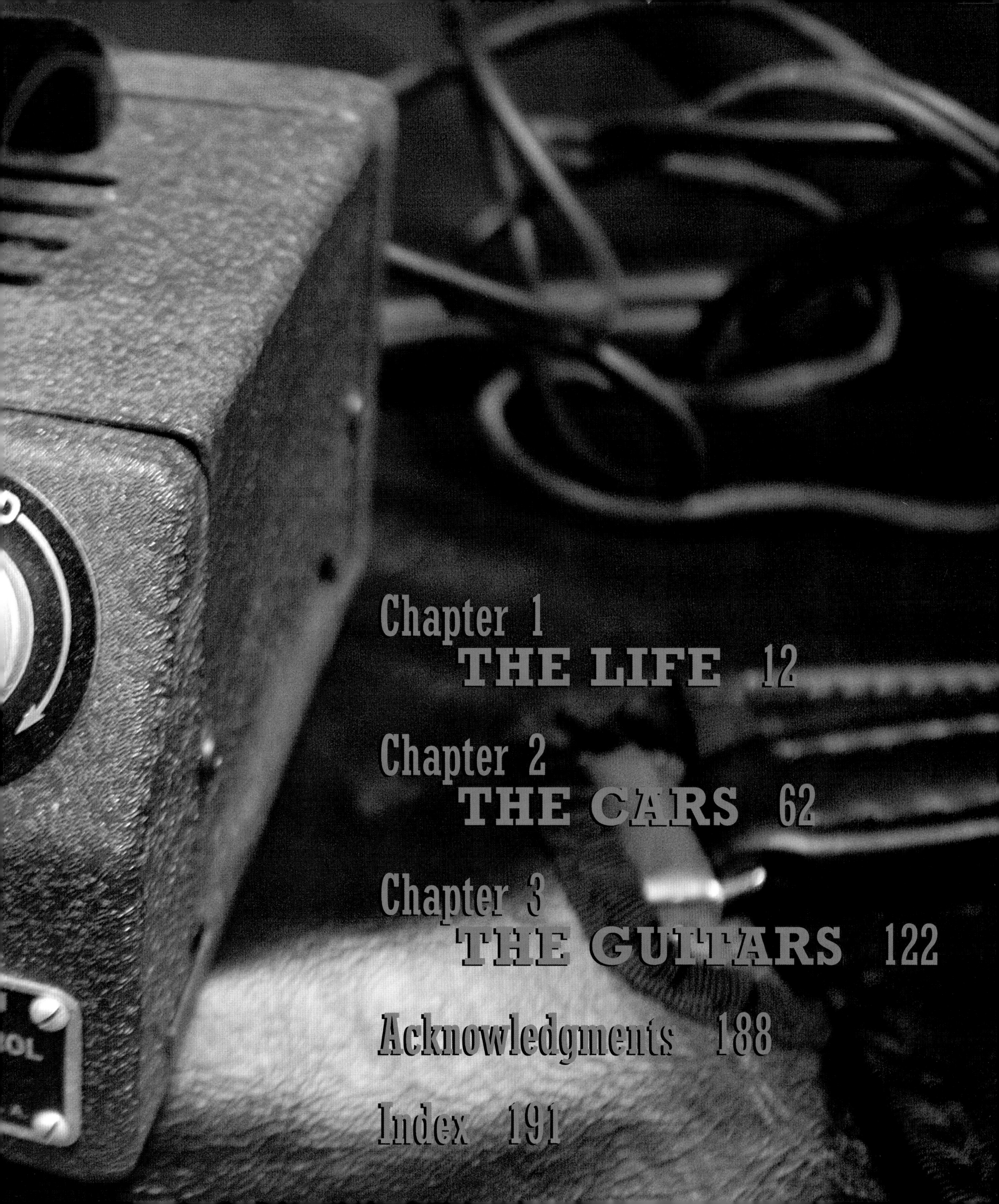

This tale of Billy F Gibbons just might as well begin right here ... we go down deep back into Houston, Texas ... and down deep it goes in Houston High Society and thru the shotgun shack neighborhood known as Houston's Fourth Ward. For it's a tale of some of Mr. G's most important beginnings ... Family and the stuff called Rock 'n' Roll. Here 'tiz ...

THE LIFE

WELL, LET'S SEE . . . THAT TEXAS THING REMAINS THE BIG PICTURE, always a place to call home.

In addition to the family—sister Pam, the Mom, and the Dad—this life remains cast with a host of characters, some famous, some yet to become famous.

Along with the family, friends, and this everlasting cast of characters, "Big Stella Matthews," caretaker of the chillun and affectionate educator in the unexpected wild world of Blues, Gospel, and Rock 'n' Roll, enters the early picture, teachin' a crash course in good, good times. "Big's" oldest daughter, "Little Stella," barely 18, liked to take us for a night stroll 'round the nightclubs after we were supposedly tucked-in for the night. But down the street and 'round the corner on West Gray laid some of the most amazing joints around, you know—The El Conquistador, Matt Garners' Place, The Right Spot Lounge, along with a few neighbors' houses—just where the nighttime good times were jumpin'. And, as you might guess, we were most assuredly thrillin' and downright mesmerized by these unexpected surprises.

Little sister Pam and I stayed two or three nights a week down in Fourth Ward with Stella. She looked after us and we learned the art of kinda fittin' in. It was different from our folks' house, but we liked it—particularly when Little Stella would slip us out!

Seein' what we saw, hearing what we heard, you knew that something was right here, right now. Passion to the marrow, even as young 'uns. What follows is what was about to happen.

As mentioned, the local live show scene . . . Man! So mind-blowing, each night an experience with loud music, another notch in the axe handle. Radiating! And, to add fuel to the fire, vinyl records, the mighty platter of wax, appeared. Most importantly, the experiences expanded: seeing live performers in person, then reliving 'em and replaying 'em thru the mystery of that spinning vinyl disc.

Needless to say, these were cornerstones of what I wanted, inspiring me to begin playing and learning the kind of music I wanted to hear.

Next move? Christmas Day in '63, that first guitar showed . . . *ELECTRIC GUITAR* at that! Within about half an hour, I had "What'd I Say," Ray Charles' famous one, and a couple of Jimmy Reed's tunes down good.

Willie Davis, yardman and slam man. As Willie said, "I can show ya . . . but you got to go ya."

As soon as I picked up that primitive Gibson Melody Maker, single cutaway, single pickup, sunburst finish, and a Fender amp, you just couldn't stop me. Still got one, still remember my first few licks on it, still remember puttin' the amp in the window, aimed down the street!

Indeed, call it a lightning bolt or whatever . . . it struck brightly then and keeps on striking. Sometime in the same place, sometime in the same manner, and when guitar's in hand, look out! It's off and runnin'! Hard focus and vision, I guess—I just know it started, don't exactly know when it's to be complete, it's simply a driving force that keeps me going. It's those early influences and elements still woven thru the fabric, from the get-go to the present.

Two guitars and drums, plain and simple . . . turn 15 and turn it up! The Coachmen, left to right: V. E. Harris, BFG, and V. E.'s brother, Virgil.

The Coachmen complete with continental ties. Take note, BFG (second from left) playing the plank that started it all, the '62 Gibson Melody Maker, still floatin' around somewhere under the name "Easy Pickin'."

THIS TEXAS THANG

Now then . . . Texas. Texas is a most unusual place. Right smack in the middle of ever'thing, both the flashiest top and the funkiest bottom—like a groove funnel. The range and variety, from C&W, to deep, dark down-and-dirty Blues, thru the shifting sands of, you know, Tejano and Mexican border music, all kinds of music, it'll getcha every time. It's . . . well . . . overwhelming. Way much coming atcha all the time. Try it sometime. Get in the car, turn the radio up, and you'll probably find a little anything and a lot of everything. It's 24 hours a day, a nonstop barrage of delight.

I'll start with the Mexican influence. In almost every Tex-Mex haunt—café, club, or the corner hangout—there's always some Norteno sound in the air, on the jukebox and in your head. It's like a good, spicy hot sauce, and that is a good thing! Music from the Tex-Mex border—that foreboding cactus zone—carries a familiar blues-like architecture. Blues and Spanish fitting together in a fine, likeminded manner. They're cut with the same feelings.

And speaking of feeling, Houston's big-tower radio stations—KILT, Houston's black radio, KYOK, and KCOH—they split the airwaves with the rockin' stuff, too. And the personalities! Dizzy Lizzy, Sister Sue, Perry "Daddy D" Cane, Skipper Lee Frazier, Jim Wood . . . these cats walked and talked with a power, this was some stylin' broadcast blastin'. They brought the message thru town. You couldn't escape it. Who'd wanna?

And the nightclubs: Don Robey's famous El Dorado Ballroom with his Duke and Peacock record labels. Ray Barnett's Fabulous Cinder Club. Club Paradise. The Palladium Ballroom. Jimmy Menudis' Showbar. The Lean-2. North Shepherd's In Crowd Lounge. The Jensen Drive–Lyons Avenue strip. The Shamrock. The Tidelands . . . if ya wanted Blues, ya got it. This was the mid-60s place to be. Check it out: B. B. King (with his hand-picked lineup outta the H-town inner circle), Piano Slim, the James Brown Revue, Howlin' Wolf, Albert Collins, Albert King, Freddie King, T-Bone Walker, Jimmy Reed, Gatemouth Brown, Widemouth Brown, Muddy, Big Walter the Thunderbird, Lightnin' Hopkins, Clifton Chenier, Grady Gaines with Little

Richard, Bo Diddley, Chuck, Hop Wilson, M. L. Martin and the Loverboys, Cookie and the Cupcakes, Bobby Bland, Little Junior Parker, Big Mama Thornton. This is just for starters, mind you!

And the hillbilly infusion . . . Strong! Bill Quinn's Gold Star Records lineup of stars, Big "D" Records, Jay Miller's Gold Band label out of Louisiana, from the Gulf Coast, thru Lake Charles, Lafayette, St. Martinville, Eunice, Big Mamou, Red Stick, New Orleans, "Loosierana," up the road to Mississippi, and all points in between with their own distinct sound/style. Killer!

'Bout this time, I was also starting to play around with that Melody Maker. I joined my first band, The Saints, when I was just turning 14—had about a six-month stab at it to get it together. My pals, Steve Mickley, Phillip Taft, and David "Feedback" Crosswell, got it goin'. Three guitars and a drum kit, that was all there was to it. But, man, it was a band. What a blast! Now I was hooked. Many a night we wound up skinning over a back fence with guitar in hand, chased by the heat, but that's what it's sorta all

Pre-bearded Willy wailing with his Ten Blue Flames.

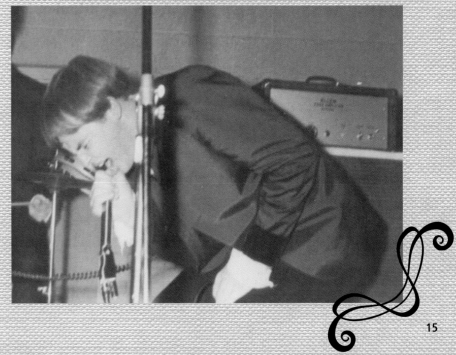

The Moving Sidewalks blazing in blazers! Left to right: D. F. Summers, BFG, D. M. Mitchell, and Tommy Moore.

16

about. Doin' the do . . . and doin' the don't too! I belonged to the band, and it's been that way ever since.

The Saints' lineup around '66 got bigger and mo' bigger. The next outfit, Billy G. and The Ten Blue Flames, made style with the hottest of soul revues: G. G. Shinn and the Roller Coasters, Jerry "Count" Jackson and the Boogie Kings, Cary Rey and the National Soul Revue, Joey Long and the Tearjerkers. You know, the Stax Records Memphis sound, the Muscle Shoals Fame Studios sound . . . they kinda ruled the world. Otis Redding, Eddie Floyd, Percy Sledge, Garnett Mimms, James and Bobby Purify, Wilson Pickett, Rufus, Carla, Eddie Floyd, Bunker Hill, Don Gardner and Dee Dee Ford, Mack Rice, Isaac, Booker T., Aretha . . . R&B was keeping the good thing on the deck.

The English outfits were hittin' too. Trimmin' the band to a small combo 'twas the way, José! Three guys makin' a bare bones go of it . . . guitar, bass, drums—that was it! A keyboardist with a Hammond B3 solidified The Moving Sidewalks. I was holdin' down the guitar and vocals, D. F. Summers on bass, Tommy Moore on B3, D. M. Mitchell on skins. The Sidewalks—originally cutting for Tantara Records, brothers Steve and Richard Ames' label, right down the street—worked good. Our song "99th Floor" hit, then was leased to, oddly, the soul/R&B label Wand Records out of New York (home of "Louie Louie," the garage rocker deluxe by The Kingsmen). "99th Floor" hit with just enough horsepower to get us in gear.

The Sidewalks were heavily influenced by them bad Brit boys, The Rolling Stones, and especially them South Texas boys, Roky Erickson and The 13th Floor Elevators. With that, The Sidewalks emerged from R&B and into psychedelia, a more experimental sound with new stuff—new gear, different effects, things to step on, things to plug into. And strange new visions . . . things altering one's mind, so to say . . . you know.

And like most everyone else at the time, there was a fresh fascination with flash. The Sidewalks particularly preferred splashy pyrotechnics. I remember driving down Highway 59, going to play a show way in South Texas, shooting bottle rockets outta the band car and generally making trouble as we went. We were racin' the road and makin' tracks. Well, somehow in this blaze of sparks, an errant firecracker flew out the window, then back *IN* the window, and right back into the entire pack. Imagine 144 flaming Black Cat Specials poppin' off at 90 MPH. You can guess the rest. We escaped, but the car burned to the ground. We crawled from the wreckage, abandoned the burning hulk of our trusted band bus, and took to hitch-hiking to the gig. Luckily, the gear had already arrived in place. Hard to believe, but we made the show.

This is to certify that

_____

IS A MEMBER OF

THE MOVING SIDEWALKS FAN CLUB

_____

DATE _____ APPROVED BY _____

Moving Sidewalks fan club. Wanna join? Fill in the blanks . . . see ya at the gig!

Sidewalks evolution, left to right: D. M. Mitchell, BFG, Miguel Frazier, Bobby "Blue" Braden, and Adrian Sexias shakin' a tail feather.

SUMMER OF '67

Now our four-piece combo got a little tougher and harder-edged. We followed The Elevators, more often than not, like zombies on TNT, everywhere they worked. They came from the unlikely South Texas towns of Beeville and Kingville, down in the mesquite desert. With the arrival of The Elevators, there must have been a snap cosmic charge through the ozone, sending psychedelic waves around the planet, and Texas, of all places, did not get left out. When The Elevators appeared on the scene, their first single, "You're Gonna Miss Me," featured Roky's off-the-planet, blood-curdling, screaming voice, Tommy Hall's mystic, otherworldly visions, and the band's stately R&B rhythms, provoking a totally unsuspected, first psychedelic aggregation. With their first LP, *The Psychedelic Sounds of the 13th Floor Elevators*, heaven and hell broke loose and on fire with a sound message. Tommy Hall playing electric jug, Roky on guitar and vocals, lead guitarist Stacy Sutherland, drummer John Ike Walton, and Benny Thurman on Fender bass. The Elevators definitely epitomized psychedelic head spaces. They were coming on strong and thinking deep, seriously artistic, ferocious, and with passionate ideologies. That's when psychedelia took to the "real."

The 'Vators took residence in an old downtown Houston Victorian mansion, split into lofts, called the Louisiana House. Some friends and I followed suit, moved in, and started experimenting in illogical writing, drawing, recording, and unorthodox soul-searching, reaching for this suspect energy in any tangible form we could score. The place was glowing like the iris of a light ball. Summer of '67.

It might be fair to say the beat on the street looked beyond "predictable-ness" and into something completely unknown, heading into personal experiments . . . visions of higher power. Doors of perception, expanded consciousness—this was *activité du jour*, day-by-day, hands-on, full-blown. Sort of, "We don't know where we're going . . . we're going there anyway." With The Elevators at the forefront, we made way to go to California. We went in a hopped-up Pontiac GTO, hitched up a gear-haulin' trailer, and trucked out to L.A.

The scene in Hollywood was really abuzz, really insane. We cared not. The heart of the clubs along Sunset Boulevard was such that you could barely squeeze down the sidewalk, could hardly move, yet nobody could be more free. The strip was jam-packed 24/7, four deep on the street and moving in both directions. Gazzarri's, the Galaxy, Pandora's Box, the Starwood, Doug West's Troubadour, house parties in the Hills . . . all starting to happen, a real ignition point. I kinda knew my way around and we decided to just pull up to the curb, unload the gear, and start pushing it into a club. We shoved into the Galaxy, plugged in before anybody knew what was up. The house management said, "Who are these guys?!"

So, with a "You got it" from the management, we landed the gig. They kept us for a time at the Galaxy and at Gazzarri's, which were going strong, and we stayed on, layin' down the sound. These were really underground days—playing after hours, playing any hours (!), just playin', playin', playin'. Groovin' on more things than one.

Moving Sidewalks at the Teen Age Fair. If you a teen, come make the scene!

THE
MOVING
SIDEWALKS
SCEPTER-WAND RECORDING ARTISTS
Houston TEEN-AGE
FAIR 1967

Psych-out, Sidewalks style. Above: BFG, Tommy Moore, D. F. "Fright Wig" Summers, and D. M. Mitchell. Right: A Hendrix-era look at the Moving Sidewalks in session.

TOUR TIME

Sometime later, around '67-'68, an agent back in Texas sent us a call from Chas Chandler, former bass player from The Animals. Now the manager of the Jimi Hendrix Experience, he was requesting a booking on their upcoming tour. We knew Jimi and Noel Redding and Mitch Mitchell were inventing another strong, three-piece tradition. They would drive that trio like it had never been done before. It was just remarkable what they did. They wanted to place The Sidewalks on the bill. As The Experience Tour was coming west, we picked up with Jimi in Texas, and played the opening night in Dallas.

I recall checking into the hotel on Stemmons Freeway the night before the first show and, as it turned out, I was in a room right across the hall from Jimi and company. This was my first meeting with these enigmatic figures. Jimi had ordered up a large console record player for his suite. As the machine arrived for load-in, I got my first glance of Jimi Hendrix. I had already started attempting to stylize after him, his great percussionist and drummer, Mitchell, and his rock-solid bassman, Redding, 'coz I just fell out when they released *Are You Experienced*? What a combo. Unforgettable to this day!

When Jimi gave me a nod out of his doorway, I nodded in response. His door was open and the next thing I noticed he was listening to *Truth*. I walked in and said, "Is that Beck?"

He said, "Yes, come on in . . . Dig . . ."

We both were fascinated with Jeff Beck's incendiary, wicked six-string thrashing. Hendrix . . . well, it was the most interesting, relaxed presence of power, observing Jimi doing things to a guitar definitely not designed to be done, inventing ways of making a guitar behave that no one else had yet to do. An eye-opening experience of guitar genius.

Then the tour. The tour was killer. The lineup was set with The Sidewalks, the avant garde trio The Soft Machine, The Chessmen, and Jimi as headliner. There are rumors about bootleg recordings from the tour lurking about somewhere. Some off-the-wall, renegade jam sessions. No doubt, that'd make good listening. I know I'd dig it!

I was keeping a respectful space to observe the creativity emanating from this otherworldly guy. He was so artistically driven from deep inside. One night, after a show, there was quite a bit of after-hours excitement. Pacing about with no place to go in mind. The performances were so electric, none of us could sleep long after the shows closed . . . just so on edge. Nigel, Jimi's loyal roadie, had gone out and come back with these Buick-sized sheets of paper—I think they were from a billboard company—and he climbed up and hung 'em back of the stage. And at that time, since there was no such thing as a curfew, you could stay in the building as long as you wanted, and I remember it being very late, like 3 o'clock in the morning, and Jimi called me aside and said, "Don't leave just yet, we're going to do something."

I noticed that the wall of Jimi's amps was still plugged in, standing before this giant, white paper backdrop, and from out of nowhere came these buckets of fluorescent paint, gallons and gallons of blue, red, this greenish-yellow fluorescent paint—and Jimi, with his stack of Stratocasters, handed me one and I said, "Well, man, it's upside down," and he said, "Well, man . . . let's play it."

With that, Nigel came out the other side, from nowhere, with these oversized Bahaman sea sponges and rubber banded 'em to the ends of the guitar necks. Jimi whipped up his famous feedback, playing just electronic noise—more feedback, wiggle stick, tremolo, dive-bomb sounds, electronic chaos—and we began lunging these guitars down into these paint buckets, making these rude noises and sloshing and dashing this paper behind the amps, smearing it with these colors under black light. It got so surreal so quickly, so totally off the wall . . . you don't need anything at moments like that . . . just pure, raw energy. That night was a rare and most interesting evening, not much sleep, just runnin' on raw.

KAYC got the better end of this deal!

CONTRACT

THIS CONTRACT for the personal services of __The Moving Sidewalks__

made this __1st__ day of __February_____, 1967, by and between the undersigned employer (hereinafter called the _____ and __The Ames Agency of Houston_____ (hereinafter c

It is mutually agreed between the parties as follows:

WITNESSETH:

THAT the Employer hires, through Agent, the designated performers severally on the terms and conditions spec represents that the performers designated have agreed to be bound by said terms and conditions including those hereof et Terms and Conditions." The performers have severally agreed to render collectively to the Employer their services as entertainment group known as __The Moving Sidewalks__

as follows:

NAME, EXACT ADDRESS, AND CITY OF PLACE OF ENGAGEMENT: __City Auditorium__

DATE(S) OF EMPLOYMENT: __February 3, 1968__   __Beaumont,Texas__

HOURS OF EMPLOYMENT: (Specify No. and length of sets; time beginning and ending) __One (1) 30 Minute Set__   __2:00 to 4:0__

STAGE REQUIREMENTS: (Including adequate wiring, lighting, etc.) IF NORMAL REQ. CK.

SPECIFY OTHER CONDITIONS PERTINENT TO ENGAGEMENT:

Alcoholic Beverages Served ☐ Yes ☒ No   Formal ☐   Informal ☒   Approximate Age Group Attending: __Mixed__

TYPE OF ENGAGEMENT: (Specify whether private home, public club, open dance, auditorium, stage show, banquet, c

FULL PRICE AGREED UPON: $ __Benefit__
__0 Dollars__

All payments shall be paid by certified check, money order, personal or company check or cash as follows:

(A) $ __XXXX__ shall be paid by Employer to and in the name of Artists Agent, Ames Agency, not later than
(B) $ __XXXX__ shall be paid by Employer to Artist at the conclusion of said engagement.

The signatures of the parties hereto shall constitute this a binding agreement between them.

ACCEPTED AND AGREED TO:
WITNESS MY HAND THIS THE _____DAY OF_____ 196____

X_____
Authorized Agency Representative and/or Artists Leader

WITNESS MY HAND THIS THE _____DAY OF_____ 196____

__Al Caldwell__
Employer's Name

Return all signed copies to Agent:
THE AMES AGENCY
P. O. BOX 252
BELLAIRE, TEXAS 77401
AGENCY TELEPHONE NUMBER: 622-0727 (AC 713)
NEW ASSIGNED NUMBER
621.43.13

X_____
Employer's Signature

__c/o KAYC Radio__
Street Address

__Beaumont__   __Texas__
City   State

_____
Employer's Telephone Number

THE ABOVE SIGNATURES CONFIRM THAT THE PARTIES HAVE READ AND APPROVE EACH AN "ADDITIONAL TERMS AND CONDITIONS" SET FORTH ON THE REVERSE SIDE HEREOF.

BIRTH OF THE SOLO

Following the summer of '67, things started heatin' up on every artistic level imaginable, especially the return of a real eye-opening appreciation for the Blues art form. Guitarists like Mike Bloomfield and Elvin Bishop, stepping out with Paul Butterfield Blues Band, were spotlighting the power of guitar soloing. Along with Hendrix, Clapton, Peter Green, Mick Taylor, bands like Fleetwood with Jeremy Spencer, Bloodwyn Pig, Jethro Tull . . . these influential instrumentalists were among the firsts to deliver long, extended bluesrock solos, bending strings in the fine Louisiana/Mississippi/Chicago/Texas traditions, using feedback (which had once been an unwelcome annoyance) in mesmerizing, magnetic deliveries. There was now a new world and we decided to chase down the originators, the inventors: Robert Johnson, Skip James, Robert Junior Lockwood, Mississippi John Hurt, Houston Stackhouse, Fred McDowell, Son House, Muddy Waters, Albert King, Freddy King, Albert Collins . . . the list goes on.

Keep in mind the time frame—what was happening here was echoed in the U.K. and we were all soon direct-hit by the British. The Rolling Stones were playing Muddy Waters and Chuck Berry numbers. You had The Pretty Things and The Animals, tough little combos that were really making some noise—and good noise it was. It lifted the curtain, highlighted and spotlighted the music that had been ignored for a while in the U.S. but had not been forgotten. It's not uncommon even today to find people who believe that a number of blues songs were written outside the States, when in fact, they were sitting in our backyard all the while.

Once you start peeling the onion, you realize, layer after layer, that there's something there, and it gets sweeter and sweeter as you go. Collectors who instinctively kept their rarities intact, recordings from back to the '20s and '30s . . . this cool stuff was to serve as the backbone not only to my playing, but to other guitarists here and in the rest of the world. The work of Eric Clapton, Jimmy Page, Keith Richards, and Taj Mahal was earthshaking, the dexterity that Jeff Beck was engaging in was nearly unfathomable. They were all reinterpreting the Blues for their fancy—I couldn't help lookin' at it really hard.

T-O-N-E

And it's all because of that electric guitar . . . the leap forward in redesigning the electric guitar made this crazy thing a very important tool for expressiveness. It became the special instrument with which to make some knocked-out statements—unique wranglings from the sublime to the surreal. Also, the quick rise of instrumentalists that started preferring the electric guitar as their weapon of choice helped it become a palette for making sounds that had never been heard before. It was free-form fingering, coupled with seriousness, and developing technical styles to back it up. Now it was reliable.

T-O-N-E. It's a big thing! Having grown up in the heat of it, I made it my personal determination to maintain a delivery like the same heroes that are talked about by everyone, everywhere, including contemporary guys like Eric Johnson and Keb' Mo', Robert Randolph and John Mayer. There is an underlying desire to maintain the special qualities of the electric guitar, a bona fide instrument with an innate, custom-made expansion system yet to see any end—it continues to go and grow.

As far as developing my tone goes, I could hear it in my head but I had to go chase it. If you can imagine it, the search becomes a real enjoyable excursion. I hear it silently first, and then, as soon as I come up against it and recognize it, I memorize it and access it at will. Then I own it and can share it . . . and that's what it's all about. Snag your piece of machinery . . . then, once you find it, it's just a matter of picking your poison and moving forward. The more you do it, the easier it gets. Just think, "I like this lick. Let's get more of those."

Early on, I realized that you enter an unpredictable zone of tone and, as time presses on, you find passion in chasing what makes guitars do what they do. Picking up on the gear side and bringing it into the technical side. Make it louder, a little more distorted, and a lot more tweaked.

FROM THE SIDEWALKS TO THE TOP

About '69, we hooked up with Billy Etheridge from Dallas. He played alongside Jimmie Vaughan and decided to join us in the bass-playing slot. Lanier Greig also joined up—an accomplished Hammond B3-ist in the Jimmy Smith mold.

At the time, I had an apartment, which, for lack of cash, had nothing on the walls but stolen "rainbow" handbills, easy to get from telephone poles and the ult' loft decor. One day I was sitting there and I noticed how these posters had been tacked up in no particular order, just covering up the walls. I looked, and at the left end of the wall was a B. B. King poster, along toward the right was O. V. Wright, and all the way over at the far end was ZZ Hill. I liked the ZZ part . . . I liked the *King* part . . . but together, no . . . too much like "B. B. King." But *King* is like the *Top*, so we changed the name of the band . . . ZZ Top!

This was another turn of events, real cool, real quick. We moved into this outland ranch where we could jam. More great times. We threw big parties, fireworks, pistol shoots, horse races, drag races, dice games, card games, wet T-shirt bashes, suds 'n' studs stripper contests, every kind of cactusland madness you can think of. Everybody havin' a go of it!

During one rare full eclipse of the moon, we held the so-called "Lunar Eclipse with th' Lunartics," a rousing ruckus. The "Lunartics" . . . what a concept! However, nonchalance being the order of the hour, our fair drummer filled up a gunpowder flash pot to celebrate the oddity of the evening and, uh, wasn't paying much attention 'bout it 'til a cigarette ash dropped dead-center into the powder keg and damn near burned the place to the dirt! Cars and guitars don't likes 'dat! Ah, yeah . . . the days at the ranch. But some good tunes came outta that, though.

One of the first-ever promo photos of ZZ Top. Left to right: Billy Etheridge, BFG, and D. M. Mitchell. Attitude incarnate . . . the party's gettin' started.

Z.Z. TOP

is like a beast on TNT
he s**y in the groove

Bill Ham and BFG. C'mere son, I'm gonna make you a star!

The three-headed monster. A very early London-era ZZ band shot

Now, somewhere there are recordings from those ranch days, totally raw, stashed away. Good Blues, I do believe. I had an old Ampex recording machine out there. Remember those things mechanics lay on so they can roll underneath cars and work on 'em? It's a thing with a neck pad and rollers . . . well, the old Ampex had long given up its wheels, so it was rolled up over an old BBQ pit on one of these mechanic's contraptions. Great place to store a piece of recording equipment, right? Well, anyway, while we were out on a road run with the band, Nolan Cheatham, the ranch hand in charge of keeping the place in order, thought the tape machine, draped over with a canvas dust-cover, was a fine, new BBQ grill. He built a raging fire underneath the old Ampex and cooked up a flame-broiled roll of recording tape. Lasted for about six minutes 'til it torched out, but, man, before it went out, we laid down some tasty licks and, finally, some damn interesting BBQ, on that machine.

This was the summer of '69, when the name officially became "ZZ Top." The drummer had the bright idea of suggesting, "Look, we got something going here, *and* we've got a management offer to contract your ZZ Top idea." The Moving Sidewalks were about to expand horizons. We remembered backing up John Mayall on one of his cross-country fieldtrips, and he liked the impromptu, laid-back Sidewalks Blues thing, so he asked us for a second

night—Mayall was on London Records, as were the Stones. London Records had global distribution and, not surprisingly, that seemed appealing. I mean, come on . . . Mayall, Clapton, Stones, Peter Green, Mick Taylor?!

Well, Bill Ham, Dot recording artist and one of Mayall's longtime friends, rang up John and said, "Hey, man, that group playing with you recently, the Moving Sidewalks, called me up about possibly contracting with one of the major labels now chasing them about. I'm sorta of interested in the group and we think joining your London labelmates might be the ticket . . . what say?"

The next day we were "ZZ Top"—this all happened within a day or so. We signed the now famous management/artist relationship with Bill and, in time-honored fashion, lighted cigars and went about designing a "Let's git it" plan.

The breath of fresh air that Bill Ham brought to the table was his interest in continuing to create a real Rock 'n' Roll legend, archiving by way of recording. He urged us to get studio-ready and off we went to Doyle Jones Recording Shop on the midtown side of Houston. Doyle ran a great analog house, and we cut a first single, "Salt Lick" b/w "Miller's Farm." It was launched, in-house, with Scat Records.

Bill Ham, moving forward, pressed our own singles 'til the London deal was complete. All eyes were on our outfit, this Texas trio. Back-to-basics,

Streakin' and freakin'

A singin', guitar-slingin' son of a gun!

minimalist, power trio stuff. I continued writing, moving from the ranch into a raunchy rent house, quite the posh crib . . . the furnishings were an electric garage door, a TV, three chairs, and some band equipment.

By this time the ZZ single began taking off, gaining goodly airplay, and the gigs rolled in, starting us from the Mexican border all over Texas.

That's when there came an important change in the ZZ Top lineup . . . namely, Mr. Frank Beard and his bandmate, Mr. Dusty Hill. As they took the stand, Beard's first words were, "I think you gonna like the backbeat," and the next day the red truck with blue-tinted windows and drums packed in every available crevice arrived at the rehearsal studio, and "Mr. Beard, the Man With No Beard" joined in with his bass-playing buddy, Dusty, whose first words were, "Hey, man, name's Dusty . . . I think you gonna like the bottom beat." We're grinnin' at each other and thinkin', "Either you know something I don't, or we're all gonna find out something we might." We loaded the gear into a transport, drove over to our favorite jam session spot, and played a Texas shuffle three hours straight, no stopping—"I'm not playing 16 bars, I'm playing 16 hours"—the Bloomfield kind of effect.

Got gear now. We made friends with Jeff Beck, hot rodder deluxe, when he was passing thru Houston and we sent him our equipment truck for a few performances. In turn, Jeff arranged a direct shipment of Marshall amps from England—two stacks (100-watt Super Leads), one for the Dust and one for BFG—the definite kick-start for our Texas trio. They appeared just as we solidified the ZZ lineup.

The gear was subsequently squeezed into our garage, and we lit the fuse and hit it for about two weeks, runnin' solid, nonstop. As the garage material was being formulated, we had our sights set on the Blues tip, interpreting it as best we could. We modernized it . . . well, we did our own version of "modernize" . . . and we definitely Texas-ized it, and we've kept rockin' it ever since.

The first ZZ Top show—in Beaumont on February 10, 1970, a booking thru Al Caldwell, the Rock 'n' Roll DJ who sponsored weekend gatherings which had caught on around the Golden Triangle of southeast Texas—is down in history as one of ZZ's most memorable gigs. As we arrived, we discovered that our fearless bass player, the bearded Dusty Hill, had spaced out bringing his guitar. We sent out the Fender-search satellite and, with much luck, our pal Steve "C" returned from his place with his Fender bass for the Dust and the show went on. With a packed house, we had a great night, playing the single "Salt Lick" and everything else we could invent on the spot. We did about an hour and a half and then shut the evening out. Really nice.

We had no rules—no nothin', 'cept goin' out to knock 'em out—and we only played the tunes we had written 'coz that's what we had in the can. We had a few extra arrangements of some shuffles, cut shuffles, and one or two slow 6/8s. We knew some Elvis songs (Dusty's mom used to say, "Let Dusty sing one! Make sure it's Elvis."), and you know, Elvis, combined with that Blues thing, was an immediate inspiration on each of us, and certainly the thing that got us hooked up.

ENTER PEARLY GATES

So we were able to get comfortable with the gear and guitars. A pivotal part of this trio has always been the upside-down style of the band . . . very low guitar and a lead-like bass, tethered together with rattly percussion. The real magical element was Pearly Gates, the 1959 Gibson Sunburst Les Paul standard. I acquired that instrument—it was found under a bed—not knowing just how vicious this guitar was made to play. It was assembled on one of those fateful days when the glue was just right, the wood was just right, and the electronics were placed perfectly. 'Til this day, I have yet to find an instrument to equal its raw power.

Pearly started shaping the sound, and, as trios go, the rhythm section, the bass and drum, gotta be solid—that and our playing style featured an automatic communication. I think of the band now as a well-oiled machine with common roots that began its unbelievable effect long before.

A pair of guitars with an incredible drum kit, a black Oyster Pearl beauty. Double kick, two toms, wrackin' snare, two floor toms . . . it was a really expressive kit. We wrenched them guitars and whacked that gear for the first five years without missing a beat.

Once we established the sound, the aim was "Don't fix it." We maintained a conviction that this was the way it was supposed to be . . . this was the way this ZZ Top thing was gelling and, really, the only change was adding more to it: from two stacks we went to four stacks, then to eight. At one point we were playing four stacks each—it was mammoth, but our band continued to chop and the recordings started poppin'. BFG and company were on the upswing and swingin' like swingsters.

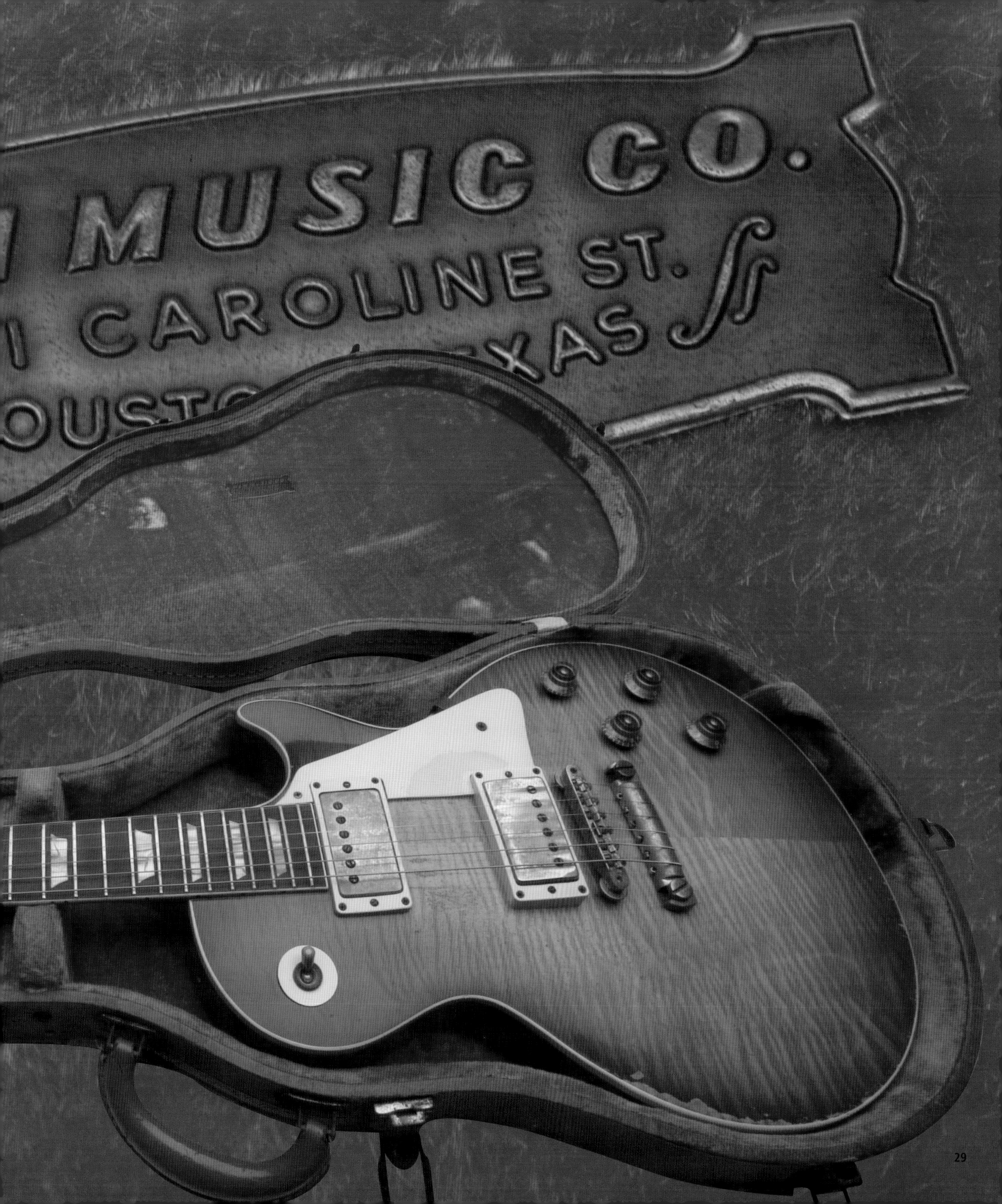
MUSIC CO.
CAROLINE ST.

THE *FIRST ALBUM* ARRIVES

The question: did the live appearances propel the sale of ZZ *Top's First Album* (1970) or was it the other way around? In some markets, the record arrived way before we did. In the summer of '70 the record got in the hands of one of our great friends and mentor, Walter Baldwin. Originally from Houston, he had migrated to Memphis.

We were recording the *First Album* when Walter rang me up, playing Peter Green's original Fleetwood Mac over the phone. It was so totally right that we raced into the studio holding on to that bit of inspiration. That was probably marked the major shift that solidified ZZ Top's personal preference: Bluesrock in the abstract.

When the recordings were completed and delivered, Walter Baldwin played a test pressing to the promoter Stedman Mathews, who was assembling the Memphis Blues Festival in the Overton Park Band Shell, still one of the all-time great venues. Stedman assumed ZZ Top was an amalgamation of black musicians. He hired us and our Memphis arrival was greeted with a great amount of curiosity—"Who are these three white guys?!" The first ZZ gig in Memphis. We had done Texas, Louisiana, Mississippi, even as far as California, but Memphis had a flavor of funk which defied description. Kinda like New Orleans. Kinda like Hong Kong. Memphis made its mark on the band . . . somethin' we would find out later.

Back to Texas . . .

Pancho's Mexeteria in Tyler, Texas, was adjacent to the recording studio named after its owner, Robin "Hood" Brian. We had selected Robin Hood's 'coz of its reputation for fine recordings and tons of R&B. Loads of hits cut for Stan Lewis' Jewel Records in Louisiana, as well as some super rock stuff released from his "outback shack." And Robin Hood knew his way around the control room. Anyway, we were hard at it but decided that since it was New Year's Eve, we should take a holiday from the session. Being as impetuous as they come, we were far too reckless to sit still, so we went next door to Pancho's, had the gear set up, and played.

Who would have thought that Pancho's Mexeteria was *the* place to hang out on New Year's Eve? But out there, there ain't much else to do. ZZ Top was up for it for sure, so away we went—'til two in the morning. The place only held 200 or 300 people, but it was packed . . . nobody went home! We added some extra sauce and everybody had a ball.

We had a bunch of cool gigs around this time. "Salt Lick" was still on the charts as we stalked bookings and found us a local dance hall in Alvin, Texas. The equipment was properly set up, the guitars tuned, the drum kit set, the curtain opened . . . and we were staring at the *one* paying customer. We said, "Well, the show must go on." We did the first set and took a break. We sent for our *one* paying customer to join us, bought him a Coke, and went out and played another set. Now that's show biz. We've kept in contact with this great guy ever since, that *one* paying customer. We couldn't figure out why nobody came 'til we got a copy of the announcement card that read, "Bizzy Top from Salt Lake." Ah, well.

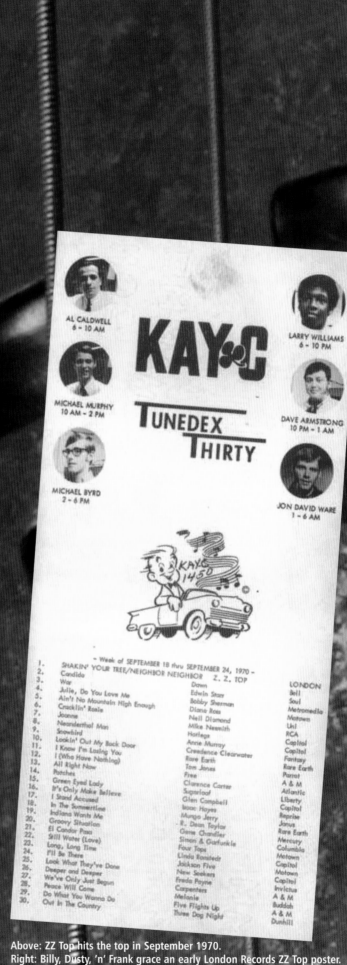

Above: ZZ Top hits the top in September 1970.
Right: Billy, Dusty, 'n' Frank grace an early London Records ZZ Top poster.

SEPT. 19-25, 1970

1 **GROOVY SITUATION—GENE CHANDLER—MERCURY**

2 Ain't No Mountain High Enough—Diana Ross—Motown

3 Julie, Do Yo... ...y Sherman—Metromedia

4 Joanne—M...

5 Candida—D...

6 Lookin' Out ...ater—Fantasy

7 Cracklin Ro...

8 (I Know) I'...

9 It's A Sham...

10 Long Long ...

11 25 Or 6 To...

12 That's Whe... ...n

13 War—Edwi...

14 Hi-De-Ho...

15 Don't Play ...

16 Patches—C...

17 It's Only M...

18 In The Sum...

19 I (Who Ha...

20 Closer To Home—Grand Funk Railroad—Capitol

21 Shakin' Your Tree—Z. Z. Top—London

22 Express Yourself—Charles Wright—W B

23 We Can Make Music—Tommy Roe—A B C

24 Everything's Tuesday—Chairman of Board—Invictus

25 I've Lost You/Flip—Elvis Presley—R C A

26 Out In The Country—Three Dog Night—Dunhill

27 Down By The River—Buddy Miles—Mercury

ZZ, Chuck, and Bo... gettin' ready go.

CHUCK, BO & JANIS

"Package tours" were the big draw when ZZ Top got together. Specialized head-line tours would come later. So the first couple years of our road trips were to small bars and hangout joints mixed in with package revues—these were usually four or five bands, each doing their few hit songs and that was it. We played with a lot of other Texas acts like Roy Head, Sir Doug Sahm, Sunny and The Sunliners, C. L. Weldon, The "Treat Her Right" Traits, Jesse Langford, Dean Scott . . . all great players and singers.

We did a stint early on backing up Lightnin' Hopkins, Freddie King, Jimmy Reed. Both Chuck Berry and Bo Diddley paid us to be their backup band for a few shows. We'd stretch out, doing a full hour show to open, then stay onstage for the Chuck Berry performance, and close the night out with Bo Diddley. They would switch headlining every other night—Bo, then Chuck.

Neither kept a setlist. It was really twisted 'coz they expected us to know every single song in their repertoire. They would just call out tunes . . . hell, songs that didn't even have names! Completely off the cuff. They might play a verse, solo, then we'd have to fall in line and finish it out.

"What key?"

"Uh, 'G-demolished.'"

But we learnt how to perform in that Rock 'n' Roll-meets-Blues style.

It was during this time that Bo gave me the "Jupiter Thunderbird," one of his self-designed guitars. Of course, Bo was already known for his square guitar, but in 1959 Gretsch had custom-made a couple more of Bo's unusual designs, including the Jupiter Thunderbird. That fine guitar is another real cornerstone instrument. (It's now in the Gretsch line, known as the "Billy-Bo," a real Killerdiller! Read all about it in Chapter 3.)

In addition to Chuck Berry and Bo Diddley, we did some early dates with Janis Joplin and Big Brother and the Holding Company. I think we did about 20-odd shows, a bunch of venues, Albuquerque, Phoenix, Tucson, out to Nevada, and all the way to Seattle. Once we connected, we made the road rounds, eventually making way back to Texas. At one particular show, some crusty lyrics of ours offended someone in the audience. Before we knew it, in the middle of our set, a dozen uniformed police appeared on stage to take us down. Janis heard the commotion and came to the rescue. She refused to go on 'til they let us go. We were turned loose and she put her arms around us and spirited us off to her dressing room, where we had a big communal band bash. Made a Southern Man feel comfortable, if you know what I mean . . .

The Janis tour was good times, but it was also *great* work. We actually looked forward to playing wherever we were—large venues, coliseums, com-munity centers, arenas—it was becoming the new vogue: the *headlining act*. Janis and Big Brother had gone to San Francisco and released their great first record, and the resounding nature of that record endeared them to millions. Janis and Big Brother were dedicated rockers. This was when San Francisco had been established as a place where new music was being made. Bands around the Bay began launching their own tours. From inside the cramp of a Chrysler station wagon, we were getting intimate with what this thing called "touring" was all about. It inspired us to keep writing and it inspired us to get on record.

The famous Tex-Mex barroom jam. Following a stage-side invite from the doorman, the long hand of the pay palm arrived along with our bar tab . . . five bucks a pop and five times the funk. "Pay to play"? No prob!

RENEGADE RECORDING

Headline tours were a big turning point, coming to terms with *live* performing and then, the opposite, *studio* performing. Different things altogether. We were learning the studio events were the repeatable ones, mistakes and all. Makes you into a real musician, quick. Turn 180 degrees and hit the stage with a live show . . . that's a big difference, dude. The studio is very serious and demanding. Live shows . . . well they are equally serious, nightmarishly loud, but totally, totally reckless—crazed gigs, sports stadiums, Vegas casinos, careless dive barrooms, Aspen ski towns, anything-goes-town Austin, mean town Mexico City, the Viper and them Hollywood hotspots—all of 'em. We were giggin' 350-odd days a year (!) with some really wicked headliners, traveling, making touring buddies, and spreading the good word . . . always.

Indeed, by '72 our onstage skills were gettin' good and sharp. We were writing songs along the way, tellin' lies, smokin' Lucky Strikes, drinkin' good red liquor, gettin' in trouble, refining as much as we could, razor-strappin' the compositions into place, keeping it as simple as the music we listened to.

The live work had taken on such a rigorous schedule that writing (the first record was written back at the ranch) was now being done full renegade style, in the dressing room, backstage, during an afternoon sound check, in an airport, on the street corner, taxicab, backseat of a friend's car,

One of the first official ZZ Top 8x10 glossy promos, shot on the Mexican border.

Relaxin' on set . . . getting' ready to raise some sand.

Cowboys and log cabins . . . the moon shines inside.

on a fishin' boat, everywhere on the fly! Pretty much us three, writing while movin' down the road. Management was good at creating writing session breaks from the road to the studio. And this we did—back to record our second album, *Rio Grande Mud* (1972).

With the release of *Rio Grande Mud*, we got lucky, catching on in places that had previously been considered quite remote. Somethin' was happenin'. We enjoyed it and kept on rockin', touring incessantly and headlining the new ZZ Top show.

Tres Hombres (1973) clearly defined the Texas boys . . . sort of that Texas-built braggadocio, that "it's bigger and better" Texas thang. Meaning, "I can drink more beers, herd more cattle, drive faster cars, got more hats," that whole chink of humor.

We got Leo's Mexican Café to prepare a heapin' platter of enchiladas then completed recording that third disc and took it on down up to Ardent Studios in Memphis and hired the house mixologists to work it. That got us our first Top 10 single, "La Grange," recorded as an afterthought, almost an accident. We were struggling with how to perform it. So, we were taking a break, just relaxing around in the studio, and at that moment . . . one take! Total boogie, coupled with a sly reference, in the fine ZZ Top tradition, to a seductive and somewhat secretive Texas country club. That one take was the keeper. place that track as our breakthrough release.

But, hey! La Grange indeed is a Texas tradition. Dating back to the '30s, it remained "private property" with Texans 'til it flourished and came to attention around the planet. It was a place to drink, it was a place to hang out . . . then brag to your buddies you'd been a good Texan. The EighthWonder of the World. I just love that one!

After that came invitations for appearances, building customized touring sets—the ZZ touring map expanded geometrically, covering all four corners of the U.S. From '73 to '76, we toured nonstop. Three hundred fifty days on the road a year for three outta-control years. A grueling, gruesome experience, that manner of madness, yet the taste, the feel, the range of this crazy place called the U.S.A. . . . too mucho coolest, mi 'migo!

Next came *Fandango!* (1975), half of it recorded live at a gig at the Warehouse on Tchapatoulas Street in New Orleans. We hooked up with the Allman Brothers and Quicksilver Messenger Service for a swoop thru the Southern states, making a stop in New Orleans' famed Warehouse. As soon as we settled in, a humongous hurricane swept thru the Gulf Coast, hitting square dead center of New Orleans—and dead center over the club, blowing the entire roof off the building. While The Allman Brothers and ZZ Top were holed up, trapped inside, boards were flying off the walls and windows were popping out. It was decided that there was nothing else to do but sit it out. We knew showtime would come soon enough so we could blow the roof off again! The shows were delayed, but the card games and hurricanes were not! The arrival of good weather made for some lathered bet-makers the night of the first show after the storm, but the show must go on! All true (we think).

During that squall, a sound truck loaded with recording gear took refuge from the storm inside the Warehouse—an eighteenth-century building, right on the Mississippi riverbank with oversized cotton-wagon doors. So we all sat on the edge of the stage, tellin' lies, burnin' smokes thru the night, and within 24 hours the lights came back on

Houston Liberty Hall. Play it, John Hammond . . . I'll play it too!

A cavalier BFG with a Louisiana invitation, featuring MC Sugar Coated Sugar Bear.

and the building was patched up. The crew that repaired the joint also did some quick 'n' dirty repair work on the mobile truck that had driven in to get outta the storm.

The recording techs said, "Now, wait a minute. Aren't you the ZZ Top guys?"

The chief engineer asked, "Do you mind if we set up, help you out a little bit, and get the gear back in order?" Before we knew it, the show was going down, tape was rolling, and that's how that happened in '75. The name of the storm? . . . don't care to remember!

Let me also state, *Fandango!* stands as an interesting disc because it came in the heyday of the two-side vinyl L.P. The A side, in this case, being the live side, backed with five studio tracks on the flip, including Dusty's fine work on "Tush."

Below: No explanation necessary!

Above: A Sunset Strip billboard announcing the big show at the L.A. Forum.

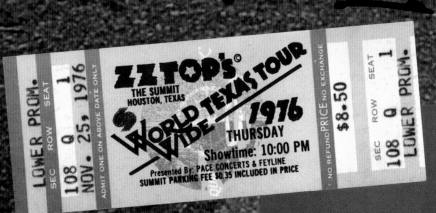

A rare and untouched ticket from the '76 Thanksgiving Day appearance of the Worldwide Texas Tour.

WORLDWIDE TEXAS

Around this period, we were approached by a good friend from New World, an outlandish character with a flair for the near ridiculous. His suggestion: take Texas, in its entirety, into a concert arena. We gathered with art directors and lighting directors, sound company designers. Everybody was intent on outdoing everything ever done before . . . more is better! There was a large platter on the table, so ZZ Top's Barn Dance and Barbeque, dreamed up by band, crew, management, production outfits, and other invited uninitiated souls, came up with idea after idea to launch the boldest large-scale stage production in contemporary arena-rock showtime. It was set for an appearance in Austin at the University of Texas football stadium.

We made the rounds with everyone, especially the famous Hollywood costume designer Nudie and his right-hand men, Manuel Cuevas and Jaime Castaneda. The three of them had us looking as sharp as tacks for this big gig with their renowned rhinestone cowboy suits. It was a mammoth show that featured some friends that we had made along the way—Santana, Joe Cocker, and Bad Company—and ZZ Top, the headliners. They still don't know how many entered thru the gates. Now *that* was a gig, hot and rowdy! One group even carved a giant state of Texas, by hand, out of the field's Astroturf. After the smoke cleared from that one, we were banned for life from ever stepping foot in that stadium . . . ever. What a way to go . . .

We continued with rounds of robust and rousing exchanges, and decided to take on everything with a concept for ZZ Top's Worldwide Texas Tour. "Do it all!"

"OK, we're going to cast the stage in the shape of Texas—our biggest stage ever created, angled 18 degrees 'til everybody's *in Texas.*"

"Well, what's Texas without cattle? Bring a longhorn steer and, well, we may need a buffalo . . . bring a live buffalo . . . we'll also need a couple vultures, a couple of live rattlesnakes, a javelina hog, and a couple of tarantulas for good measure."

It was the single largest undertaking that we'd been involved with, and, at the same time, it made sense 'coz now the "Lil' Ol' Band from Texas" would be "Taking Texas to the People." So this grand illusion started taking shape, and over the course of the year it began to fall in place. A fleet of semi-trucks and buses grew to move this production. Over a year in construction, thru the end of '75, fabricating inner workings, getting' it prepped to hit the road . . . it was barely manageable. The sheer enormity of it all required two touring-company packages. The Worldwide Texas Tour mainstage took two days to put up and a full day to take down. With a travel day on either side, that burned up nearly a week, so our second team was sent ahead to build the streamlined version. We did three or four nights with the stripped-down show, then played a stand with the big Texas Worldwide show, usually two or three nights for the weekend.

The full-blown dates were selective appearances just due to the monstrous magnitude, the unreal size to the extreme. And the detailing—a set-carpenter's challenge from Hell, with promises to the suppliers, unheard-of inventions for the builders, guarantees to the welders, bonuses to the

One of the many 18-wheelers custom-painted for the Worldwide Texas Tour.

electricians, backroom guarantees to the engineers, even guarantees of solace to the animal-protection groups, which meant caretakers for the ZZ livestock. Them animals had better care taken of them than anyone of us . . . or anyone else, for that matter. We got burgers, they got steak.

It all worked out, even despite a few mishaps, particularly with the live-stock. Our favorite, Buffalo Boogaloo, got loose at Three Rivers Stadium in Pittsburgh and dragged the trainer twice around the outfield, but he held on and Buffalo Boogaloo got his wings, smiling all the while! On another night, one of the vultures got loose, flying around the coliseum in Richmond, Virginia. We stopped the show for a moment as the handler came out to call him in. He'd taught the bird how to recognize his white hat, but, remember, this was at a time when white cowboy hats were popular all over the globe. The bird was trippin'! Didn't know who was who or where to go, but flyin' around the coliseum was probably good exercise. But the comeback call came shoutin' out. The guy, Ralph Fisher, "Animal Man," whistled once, tapped his hat twice, and the bird came back with a perfect, two-point landing, right on his white Stetson. A tough act to follow, to say the least. But the show goes on, my brother.

Two for the show.

A sunset stage shot view from the Worldwide Texas Tour . . . the boys are leanin' into it.

Worldwide Texas Tour . . . even the critters git love.

The Worldwide Texas Tour was a grueling grind but had its high, high moments. It was a real juggling act that was managed rather masterfully by our personal agent and by our colorful promotion man, who together orchestrated the trips from venue to venue, as well as side trips back to Memphis—now a second home there in the studio—and back to California for remaking wardrobe and redoing equipment. Then back out to the next show somewhere. This, of course, all went in keeping with the ZZ image. Lookin' shiny, slammin' loud, still playin' the famous Pearly Gates, the trusty Fender bass, and a new big-kit drum package to complement this overloaded behemoth of a production. It was quite the tour to get through.

Tejas (1976) was recorded over the course of maybe six months of that touring year. It nicely reflects the continuing evolution of the band's togetherness as writers. We were engaged in so many diverse activities, it stimulated the writing process with tales from the road. As many bands discover, the road experience is an unusual job, but it makes for some good tall tales.

Packed up tight . . . doin' it right. Billy and the boys rock the house!

EXILE

After the close of the tour, we took a six-month break that lasted three years, a self-imposed exile from the sweatshop called The Road! Frank went to the Caribbean. Dusty went to Mexico. And I moved to Europe. We were just knockin' around, experimenting with new musical horizons, different instruments, percussion sounds, different equipment. We remained "the band" by telephone, maybe the occasional correspondence or telegram, but groovin' like a touring road trip.

Once we returned together, we got back into the control room to find out where our experiments had taken hold and what the experience revealed . . . but we had to wait and see. Blind communication sometimes be a good thang! We had all gotten conveniently lazy, a bit scraggly, and grown long beards. At that time, Warner Bros. had decided to sign ZZ Top, which launched the release *Degüello* (1979).

Well, we had enjoyed a successful start with the London Records team, but it was on to the West Coast with Warners. The prowess of our new pals at Warner Bros. generated a new sense of rock, a new sense of importance . . . just making good old Rock 'n' Roll.

During a three-year absence from touring, and just about everything else, we had stumbled into a number of uplifting encounters. One righteous hang was with Bob Marley and the Wailers. The reggae players showed us how to shift a traditional three-chord standard into 12, 16, and 24 blues patterns. We took the composition side a bit closer to home. We had the good fortune of re-igniting our friendship with The Fabulous Thunderbirds, Jimmie Vaughan's great outfit bursting out of Austin, and with the killer jump-blues outfit Roomful of Blues out of Rhode Island. We also spent some time with Lightnin' Hopkins, hung around with the Rolling Stones, drove fast cars, drove faster cars, and other fast things we won't mention just yet . . .

We did move toward a larger sound and, thanks to the recording bonus of multi-tracking, our studio engineers added a soulful element into the mix. We maintained the integrity of the band, just us three guys, which forced us to learn new instruments. We had never laid a hand on some of these things, but we woodshedded 'til we got it right. We picked up playin' horn for a pair of songs written for *Degüello*. The tracks "Hi-Fi Mama" and "She Don't Love Me, She Loves My Automobile" shook the tape machine, but after several takes we grabbed it and ran with it. Extra nice. From a version of Elmore James' "Dust My Broom" to "Cheap Sunglasses." More personal favorites.

Having excursioned into some strange lands and now exchanging ideas on some new equipment, we came back to the studio totally committed. It was not predictable where the journey would wind up, but the sound that emerged was a result of traveling "outside the box." Also, keep in mind a budding new scene coming out of Georgia, with R.E.M., Love Tractor, the B-52's . . . really with it. Akron bands doing really powerful sounds. The music scene was changing and becoming more important as a cultural expression. We may have been immune to fashion, but we certainly were not immune to these musical influences. We started fooling around with different guitar tunings and microphone techniques. Things associated with live performance also connected our studio playing. We got a lot of great direction, the best . . . Joe Hardy, Terry Manning, John Hampton, and John Fry, who came from Stax. Lizzie Harrah and G. L. Moon from Houston. They were with us, getting the job done. Pure genius.

Back on the touring circuit, we took off to Europe, more weirdness, more wildness. But in our collective conscious, we still took along our influences and still take 'em along today, wherever we go . . . the bluesmen, the rockers: Jimmie and Stevie Ray Vaughan, Augie Meyer and Doug Sahm, Doyle Bramhall I & II, Cadillac Johnson, Red Pharoah, Johnny Cash, Merle Haggard, George Jones . . . Fleetwood Mac, Savoy Brown, Eric Johnson, Van Wilx, Grateful Dead, Ozzy, Prince, The Allman Brothers, Alice Cooper, Rev. Horton Heat, Los Lobos, Sum 41, Pearl Jam, Superjoint Ritual, Lynyrd Skynyrd, Thunderbirds, Paladins, Santana, Los Relampagos, Dwight Yoakam, Kid Rock, Kracker, Metallica, Los Tigres del Norte, a bunch of them crazy country cats (Oh, yeah, Townes Van Zandt . . . I once picked him out of a dumpster. I asked, "What are you doing in there?" He said, "I threw myself away. I'm just no good."), Hank Williams III, Al Jourgenson, Crystal Method, Miles, Thelonius, Johnny & Edgar, B. B., all of 'em . . . I just luv this guitar and what it does to you.

One of the standouts from *Degüello* was "I'm Bad, I'm Nationwide," which was a reference to our guitar-slingin' friend, Joey Long. Joey looked like Lon Chaney Jr. In fact, he looked like Lon Chaney Jr. *after* Chaney transformed into the werewolf. He had big hair, and he had a gorgeous, lovely wife, a blond bombshell "Barberella."

Joey didn't drive, although he always had a new Cadillac, and he didn't bother with things like a driver's license. Come on, now! Mo' important things to do beside that! He made sure he always got to the gig on time with Barberella at the wheel of some new cold blue steel like a pistol. He always got to the gigs—that was first in Joey's book.

I recall going with Joey to an annual get-together for recording artists from Houston and around the Gulf Coast . . . Jesse Langford, Jonnie Spain, who had big hits in the '50s, C. L. Weldon and the Pictures, T. K. Hulin, Jivin' Gene . . . just wonderful. Soulful singers . . . G. G. Shinn and the Roller Coasters, Jerry "Count" Jackson and The Boogie Kings, Duane Yates, Sunny Ozuna, Cary Rey

and the National Soul Revue. Man, what a lineup . . . and what great records they made! Soulful, black as night, from cut-down club combos to 18-piece weekend ambush revue bands—this *is* the consciousness and will forever remain. Man, what we learn from these cats!

Yes, these musicians enjoyed a steady wealth of recognition just within the region known as "the Houston School." And, from San Antonio south was the San Antonio School. That was basically under the ownership of Doug Sahm and Mondo and the Chili Peppers. The Houston School ran thru Beaumont, Port Arthur, all the way to Louisiana 'til Baton Rouge. Then, the New Orleans School takes over, then Memphis. Peacock Records, which later moved from Memphis to Houston along with Duke Records, operated by Don Robey, had B. B. King, Bobby Bland, Junior Parker, Willie Mae Thornton, so many of the cornerstone Blues performers that came out of Memphis, West Memphis . . .

I don't want to suggest confusion, but imagine: It's T-Bone Walker meets Cream and every Blues artist you know meets B-52's and Depeche Mode. Just a crazy collision of elements. It was uncontrolled and chaotic studio wit and excitement . . . made you make records to dig on. The Warner Bros. deal propelled ZZ Top's bluesrock to a high, high mesa. *Degüello* was the sounding board for some heavy-hittin' tracks—"Cheap Sunglasses," "I'm Bad, I'm Nationwide," the revisitation of "Dust My Broom." We also made a cover of Sam & Dave's "I Thank You," the "always-opener" on tour.

Moving on to *El Loco* (1981), that record let us continue this experimentation, navigating thru funky lands and into new mindless grooves. Secret discrete languages invented before the metal airplane, privileged piece of poetry, saying it without sayin' it.

El Loco was an offering for audience, fans, and friends who wanted their three creatures . . . ZZ Top, their aliens from some other planet. So we kept the spot, circlin' up and slammin'. The sound—rare, medium-rare, well-done, and burnin'—hung in there and cut like a knife. Check out "Heaven, Hell, or Houston." I dig gettin' on out there and makin' it sharp with the fellas.

THREE B'S

Back in 1979, following the three-year absence from touring, we had discovered lazy and not shaving make a fine combination. So in 1983, here we have this interesting and unusual appearance, and this fancy little hot rod car. Voilà . . . sprinkle some good-looking chicas into the mix, and we had the three B's—babes, Blues, and braggadociousness, all coming together thru the convenience of your own TV.

Everything came together on *Eliminator* (1983). Now we talkin' . . . a love for them wicked girls, a lust for cars. As we were striking blowtorches, repowerin' and repaintin' and hot roddin' those classic '30s Fords, we hot rodded some sounds to go right along with 'em. Little did we know a new star was on the move. One night, Mr. Beard rang thru to me and the Dust and said, "Switch on the cable . . . some new music show." Next thing we knew, we'd been up for a day and a half watchin' this new thing called MTV!

We wrapped the album, and we, Bill Ham, and our trusty roadies loaded the little bit of gear we could muster at a moment's notice and headed straight to California with the red '33. We hunkered down with our director, Tim Newman, called in the pretty girls, scribbled out a script, and shot our first video for MTV, "Gimme All Your Lovin'." What a plan . . . we were drivin' blind to the waaaay out somewhere on the high desert, clueless and without a map, lookin' for the right location, blizzard wind blowin', colder than hell . . . well, you get the picture. Anyway, we settled on the set, set about hustlin' wardrobe, settin' up with the crew, shinin' up the ride, delirious, hungry as a fried fish in saltwater, workin' 'round the clock, beatin'

Truck-bed action with band and fur from the "Legs" video.

BLACK GOLD CERTIFICATE

FIES THAT A WEALTH OF HOSPITALITY AND GOOD WILL IS TH

gnificent Empire

10

TM

THAT LITTLE OL' BAND FROM TEXAS

BLACK HUNDRE

TEXAS BUCK

48

deadlines, walkin' the set like sleepwalkers, makin' it up as we went—scene by scene! All said and done, it turned into a real alright kinda weekend! Sing it, brother! Thrashin'.

After MTV's onslaught airplay blitz, we followed with the sequel, "Sharp Dressed Man." This shoot, in deep downtown L.A., went for the all-day-all-night record (until "Legs" was released, but that's another story).

Anyway, we enjoyed the luxury of working with the same fine crew that worked on the previous video project. Great people all the way around, and talented, each and every one: from the drivers, to the kitchen crew, grips, the P.A., and, again, some superb directing from our partner in crime, Smilin' Tim Newman. I'm not sure why he always seemed up, always all the time . . . must have been the gals and the by-now famous red '33, the "Eliminator Coupe." "Sharp" was our only night-shoot video, but a sharp-dressed man goes out at night anyway, right?

It was a gas, this one. The lovelies from "Gimme"—Gina, Danielle, and Kimmie—were back, and a motley cast of revelers made for a full-blown party in progress. Yeah, it was another round-the-clock hard grind makin' it thru to the wrap, yet the video complemented a tune which represented fond memories of long nights recording back in Memphis. True to form, those Memphis times of sultry Southern evenings, dining at the dog track across the river, dancing with the chicas, makin' backroom bets with the best of 'em, all in sharp-dressed fashion, feelin' like a million . . . too much, amigo.

I guess the best songs come from the best of times! So we did another one. The guitars were stars and the car was still up and runnin'! Boom.

"Legs." The long one . . . video, that is . . . completed this series of three fine times with our pals and the pictures. Although we did a double shoot, one keeper and an extra for good measure, no one was complaining, what with three fine galfriends, a ride in "Red," and a couple of weekends from the rigors of the road. Could be the best of the three. "Legs" be standin' tall in this book, at least. And it set the tone for what we would continue to do.

During the mid-'80s timeframe, ZZ Top, embracing this "new instrumentation," maintained a typical disregard for reading manuals. The attitude was, "Don't read the manual, just turn the knobs and make loud noise." The interesting twist is that we still had one foot in the roots, another with the rest of the world, experimenting with sometimes strange, very untraditional gear. Once again, quite by accident, we made an album by mixing lo-fi and hi, and the rest is history . . . .

BRASWELL MEMORIAL LIBRARY
727 NORTH GRACE STREET
ROCKY MOUNT, NC 27804

HANGIN' WITH LESTER, BUILDIN' TH' MUDDYWOOD

It was then that we met the infamous Gretchen Barber—"Lil' GB." She turned us on to all things happenin' Austin-side, particularly the fabulous Blues Mondays at Austin's Rome Inn, a pizza house that surrendered the building on Monday nights to The Fabulous Thunderbirds, doing some of the best Blues on the authentique. She brought us together with my coauthor, Mr. Tom Vickers, the legendary Lester Bangs, and Mr. Joe Nick Patoski, who was managing Austin's Joe King Carrasco. Lil' GB and her pal "MB" (Mary Beth in *Degüello's* "Low Down in the Streets,") coaxed Lester into leaving New York and coming to, where else, but the "odd" state of Texas! His first words were not quite understandable, but, again, we're speaking about the late, great Lester Bangs.

On this uproarious excursion we took Mr. Bangs and his trusty tape machine down to the Rio Grand Valley for some hunting, fishing, surfing, sand, and sunning de la frontera. We managed to drag him down to the wharf-side departure zone with the captain of the famous offshore fishing boat *Thunderbird*. Lester sat patiently, drifting two hours offshore on the deep blue sea, when he decided to start spouting his personal commentary on everything that was happening musically as he knew it . . . or did not know it.

For Lester, who thought a gun was something you tucked under your jacket coat and pulled out only in times of trouble, this thing called sport shooting was a rather unusual turn of events. Needless to say, his charm endeared him with some sincere, new splendid friends before he departed for that crazy place New York. I'd do it again if he were still here, and so would everybody else who knew him.

But to get back to things . . . with the release of *Eliminator* we started touring exotic spots, off to England, then onward thru Europe, Russia, Japan, Asia, Africa, Australia, New Zealand, the list went on and on. This lil' ol' band from Texas wasn't so lil' any more! With the assistance of our pals— people like Eddie Gorodetski, Bob Merlis, Joe Nick Patoski—suddenly, we were going to these newfound islands of interest around the planet. Still, ZZ Top continued doing what we liked doing best, and that's playing live. Nothin' unusual 'bout that.

At the same time, we found ourselves honored sons of Memphis, Tennessee. All in all, we spent the better part of 18 years in and out of this Hong Kong of the Delta. My great pal, Mr. Tony Fortune, had been making trips from there down through the Mississippi Delta on sales calls for his famous frozen margarita drink machines. On one such journey to Clarksdale, Mississippi, he discovered a small sign staked in the ground on the edge of the highway that said, "Blues Museum. Turn Right." He told me about it, but I had no knowledge whatsoever of such place.

The following weekend, I traveled down Highway 61 with him. We found said sign and, sho' 'nuff, there was a Blues Museum. On arriving, we met Sid Graves, the director, and Jim O'Neill, founding editor of *Living Blues* magazine. That particular day, they happened to be going to the cabin where Muddy Waters grew up, on Stovall Farm.

I was fortunate enough to meet most all of the great blues cats, but my favorite was Muddy. Once we were in Burlington, Iowa, at a blues festival, and Freddie King was on the bill. Before the show, he took us down to the basement and into the dressing room where a guitar case was balancing between two chairs as a makeshift card table. Freddie walked in, opened

up his hand, full of $100s, threw down a few, and said, "Count me in, and, by the way, these are my good friends, ZZ Top." Muddy Waters picked up his cards, scraped up the money, stared at us for a second with a big smile, and said, "Pleased to meet ya." Then it was back to the card game. That was it. The best!!!

Anyway, Mr. Fortune and I went along with Sid and Jim, who made us drag home a roof beam pulled from the cabin. Damaged in a windstorm, the cabin was threatened with demolition. Well, such an important landmark was, of course, to be preserved. This seemingly insignificant, but monumentally important, piece of wood was delivered to Pyramid Guitars back in "Mem," carved into slab, glued together, and fashioned into a solid electric guitar—the "Muddywood."

MTV also stepped forward, and with the city of Clarksdale organized an afternoon party on the city plaza, a global charitable affair calling attention to the place. ZZ's donation of the guitar to Clarksdale's Delta Blues Museum helped spark interest in the museum. Today, charitable contributions from everywhere keep the Clarksdale community and the Delta Blues Museum alive and well.

ZZ TOP

HAPPY HOLIDAYS

2002

HAPPY HOLIDAYS

FROM

ZZ TOP

DUSTY

BEARDLESS

WILLY

2000

A collection of Happy Holiday
Wishes from Billy's hand.

WEIRDOES GOIN' GLOBAL

Meanwhile, ZZ Top was becoming part of the American musical lexicon. *Saturday Night Live* began a "ZZ Top for President" campaign with Father Guido Sarducci. And, in 1986, Andy Warhol and MTV hosted a floating dance-party barge and a celebrity stage for the Fourth of July Statue of Liberty fireworks celebration. The bearded weirdoes, ZZ Top, in yachting caps and white togs, played three hours of fireworks fun. Andy Warhol's comment: "Trash to the everyman, but art to the artisan. You pick it up where you find it!"

The unfolding success of the *Eliminator* album and the MTV videos painted a picture of this unusual band of derelicts from Texas for the entertainment of the world. We'd done records, tours, TV, and videos, now it was time for the movies: *Back to the Future Part III*. Writing the theme song, "Doubleback" was easy . . . becoming the picture's "town band" was easier.

Because *BTTF3* was a western, we met director Bob Zemeckis on the set in Sonora, California. We arrived around lunchtime. The entire cast was on break, which left us wandering around in a corral on the set. Mr. Zemeckis asked his assistant, Bob Gale, "Who are those bearded guys in my corral?"

Mr. Gale's response was, "ZZ Top. The guys you invited to write the soundtrack . . . the theme song."

Zemeckis asked, "Are those beards real?"

Gale said, "I believe they are."

The director replied, "We may be able to save some money on the wardrobe—get 'em into the picture." At that moment, ZZ Top became the film's "town band"!

You know, it's flashy and glamorous on camera until one breaks down. Well, sure enough, just a few lines into this particular scene, we're in place, on our mark, following Bob Zemeckis' direction into action, when out from behind camera one, the lensman calls, "Break!"

"What's up?" from the chair.

"Camera jam."

"How much time to fix it?"

"Let me look for a second here."

"OK. Let me know when it's back to and we'll go."

So about, oh, maybe an hour passed. As we waited around with everybody else, we began gettin' into a little bit of this song, then a little bit of another one, all while standing on this stage built for the scene, and then it's into another version of another standard tune, so then it's gettin' a little lively. And now a few cast members begin drifting closer to this stage area, then a few more driftin' in, and Michael J. Fox, star of the film, strolls up and asks for a request, the Hank Williams standard, "Hey, Good Lookin'," at which we looked around, grinned, and struck up the tune. By now, there's some lighthearted spiriting goin' down . . . more requests, more music, just generally the makings of a real low-down hoedown with our "town band" act in full swing. I mean, "Play that one again!" . . . "Hey Z! Do you know . . . whatever."

After close to a two-hour "set," someone finally asked, "Is the camera ready yet?"

And Mr. Zemeckis replied, "Oh, it's been ready . . . I thought I'd let everyone enjoy a little Old West party for awhile!"

Yeah, that's show biz!

SOUTHERN KOMFORT & KUSTOM KADDIE

Following *Eliminator*, *Afterburner* (1985) saw us exploring more new sounds and hangin' on to them good ol' sounds too . . . colliding in some geometric pie, delivering something the fans would enjoy. For the "Velcro Fly" video the talented singer and dancer Paula Abdul stepped forward with her graceful choreography skills and taught the three bearded weirdoes how to dance. She finally had the set contractors nail our boots to the stage and said, "Just shake!"

From *Afterburner* we released, of all things, a ballad! "Rough Boy," created during a desolate, winter rainstorm, lamenting over lost love, emerged as an oozingly slow, strongly emotional track. Mushy and gushy, rough and tough. A strangely visual, outerspace-meets-earthlove video was a bonus that accompanied this unexpected heartbreaker.

We set out on the road again, in 1987, with an Afterburner-themed stage. A giant, stage-wide Eliminator car dashboard transforming into the Afterburner cockpit, a few special effects for entertainment's sake. But in the end it was about getting back to the real thing . . . *playing*.

A few years later, Warner Bros. called for a follow-up, this one entitled *Recycler* (1990). Hats off to my dear friend and mentor, Mr. Walter Baldwin, who suggested the album speak of things so Southern—livin' off field bets, smokin' hand-rolled cigs, cotton, drivin' old cars down 49 and 61, pickin' up a sackful of tamales (the Delta kind, mind you), stoppin' at the 7-11, flirtin' with th' women, stayin' out late and crossin' the bridge and easin' down the river—just simple things. Baldwin instinctively knew re-creating something from that tradition, from that pure form, would be a welcome reality. We went about the task of replanting ourselves from the shifting sands of Texas to the red clay of the Delta . . . "My Head's in Mississippi" . . . it's got all that. The vid from that cut sees for the first time big, bad CadZZilla, hit on screen—the next-wave kustom kar. The monster Kaddie had hit the screen.

continued on page 57

JOE HARDY

Joe Hardy was chief engineer at Ardent Studios in Memphis when he first started working with Billy and ZZ Top during the recording of the Eliminator album. He has worked with them ever since as chief engineer on their recordings for nearly 20 years.

There is no set recording procedure. You can start with a guitar riff, a guitar sound, or any sound for that matter! Billy will do the craziest things that would probably drive a normal engineer nuts. He'll come in and go, "Okay . . . give me a vocal track."

I'll say, "For what song?"

He'll reply, "It's a new song . . . there's no music yet." There's no guitar, there's no key, there's no tempo, he'll just go out and start singing 'coz he has something that he thought up, usually on the way over to the studio. Sometimes we'll build a track that way.

I mean, he might come into the studio and say, "I want a snare that sounds like a car door slamming," or sometimes he'll see something and say, "I want it to sound the way that looks." That all sounds real wacky, but he has this saying, "I know it when I hear it," and as crazy as it sounds, I know it when I hear it too!

As far as the guitar parts go, you know we spend quite a bit of time on the rhythm parts because that can define the overall structure of the song. I'd say 90 to 95 percent of his solos are first take. The whole point of what he tries to do with his solos is get as close to the edge as he can, and maybe even fall off, but get right back up and on it!

It's never thought out or rehearsed. I mean, I might punch in a note or two where he broke a string or the chord fell out, but it's never planned or rehearsed. He just pulls it out of his ass. Billy's philosophy is better sorry than safe! He just goes way out on a limb every time, and that makes it real exciting and fresh because you just never know what he's going to come up with.

Billy is real knowledgeable about the recording studio and what it can do, but more importantly, what it's getting ready to be able to do. But he doesn't keep up with the specifics. He gives me absolute freedom always. I mean any off the wall, crazy thing. I'm still trying to find something that's so out there that he'll just say, "No man, that's too crazy!" That's what we do in the studio. We just try and out top each other with how crazy we can make things sound and still make them work. That's what keeps it fun and fresh.

I'll tell you, I didn't get it for a while as far as Billy's artistic vision goes. I mean, Billy thinks that Rat Fink is art, so he's into the whole California, Robert Williams hot rod art thing. People who are only semi-educated in that stuff, like me, may think it's odd, but you might find out later it's actual real art, like comic books are real art. I guess I was more of a college snob.

But anyway, I was doing one of their records and we started in Memphis and then I came to Texas. The first night I came to the hotel I was staying at in Houston, I go into my room, and Billy had somehow gotten in there and put his original art work that he had painted or drawn all over the walls, and most of it was framed.

I mean, a lot of people don't know that Billy is a great artist, whether drawing, painting, or just doodling. The guy has an incredible eye. And he also has a great sense of humor. You can tell that from the songs. It's really hard to marry humor and drawings without it coming off as cartoony. He will come up with something that is some self-referential, Dadaist stuff that's really engaging. He's really good at that. He has a great eye for colors, shapes, it's all one thing to him. In other words, I don't think a car is any different from a song or a guitar. It's all hands-on with him. There's sort of a perception of the NASCAR crowd as tobacco-chewin', moonshine brewin', you know what I mean. It's sort of a subclass. You see, Gibbons sees past all of that. I really don't think he has a judgmental bone in his body.

He's hard to define because he's unique! I mean, it's Gibbons, that's about all you can say. We have this thing amongst the studio crew--we fine each other. If you say "Gibbons" and "why" in the same sentence, it's five dollars in the jar! There really is no rhyme or reason to it.

I've never met anyone like this. I think usually to call a pop musician an "artist" is an oxymoron. Picasso was an artist. There are a lot of really good songwriters, good players who have the structure the right way, everything's nailed down just so. But Billy goes beyond all of that. It's a weird combination of brainpower because he is really smart, but when he plays a solo it just comes from his hands. There's no thought involved, it's like instinct meets artistic vision. Because, like building a car or doing a drawing, you actually have to think about it, and there is an intellectual process that has to take place. But when he plays guitar it is absolutely primal! I think Steve Ray Vaughan had the primal thing down. I mean he could just rip a lick that would kill ya, but Billy has an extra thing, the way he marries intellect with emotion.

Many people don't realize that Billy is an innocent person. Almost in a childlike way, Billy is curious about everything, every facet of pop culture. He has a voracious appetite for the popular zeitgeist, and he has an incredible ability to know what's getting ready to happen. I don't even know how to explain it 'coz it's kinda spooky!

BFG at BMG

Things were now moving forward at lightning speed with new songs and a new home label. *Antenna* (1994) was the next CD work. BMG said, "Bring on that ZZ stuff."

Strippers, Carros, Trocas, Cantinas, Chicas, Loudness, Nastiness, Texas, El Caminos, Burritos, Enchiladas, Tacos, Cabritos, Nopalitos, Rancheros, Sombreros, Oro, Naranjitas, and Cervezacitas were not to be left out! So on *Antenna* we continue our fascination with the female form and all things (make that) *things Texicano*. In the lyrics, in the stage shows, in our minds! (Or was it mindless?!) I must say there's a whole lotta love within the tantalizing Texas trio, workin' overtime and creating sounds big as the Lone Star State itself. But make no mistake, the presence of cars, guitars, and pretty girls still gets a whole lotta attention. Just listen. "Pincushion," "Breakaway," "PCH" . . . even the vid for "Pincushion" has us flyin' and dodgin' spikes and spears. Gotta luv 'dat.

On the *Antenna* stage, however, we were trapped—trapped!—up on the mic line while the girls worked the back line. Ha! Even three chords can be tough, really tough, when you lookin' over your shoulder to see what th' ZZ girls have goin' on behind that screen!

BMG release number two, one of our faves, was *Rhythmeen* (1996). The title is just that, rhythm and *mean*. This one was propelled once again with blue mystery and quirky experimentation. This particular release remains a pleasure despite the harshness of the subject matter . . . top to bottom. We had a massive time in that studio, focusing on just that mean, mean, rhythm. Also, this was first pure trio record ever produced on the Top—just three guys gathering 'round one well-placed microphone and doing it pure old-school style. I volunteered to join the production side, as a return to the roots way of making music.

Rhythmeen was recorded at John Moran's House of Funk, which had gained notoriety with Destiny's Child, Beyoncé, Scarface, Ghetto Boyz,

REV WILLY'S KILLADILLA RENEGADE GUACAMOLE

- FISTFULS OF AVO'S
- GOOD GRINDINGS OF GARLIC
- STEALTHY HELPINGS OF JALAPEÑOS
- KILOS OF QUESO
- A LOAD OF LIMES
- PACKS OF REV WILLY'S POWDERED PEPPERS
- CARLOADS OF CRISPY CHIPS
   SLICE · DICE · WHACK · HACK
      · · · SWIRL · · ·
— GET YO' GIRL AND YOU GOT IT —
REV WILLY'S KILLADILLA RENEGADE GUACAMOLE

Los Angeles location still from the filming of the "Pincushion" video.

Bushwick Bill, Master P, all of the Cash Money guys, Manny Fresh—it was quite a scene to behold! It's on the southwest side of Houston, in an unmarked kind of nonchalant setting, but Studio A, Studio B, and Studio C, and the mixing and mastering rooms, blaze. Being 'round that energy is all good.

Joe & G (Joe Hardy & GL "G-Mane" Moon) set about doing the engineering business that we knew had to be done. It's what we dig doing anyway. To be able to hang out with these interesting characters added an edge, and mucho to the recording sessions. No overdubs, no sidetracking, just pure, straight ahead, and fierce . . . deep down, dirty, trashy, easy, and fine! The drums, the bass, and the stash of Spanish six-string electrics, filtered expertly by Joe & G, made the signal path sizzle.

Following *Rhythmeen*, 'twas back on the road, but *XXX* (1999) returned us to the studio, this time into the personal and private ZZ Top recording room, the infamous Foam Box Recordings. We worked it right in time. "Poke Chop Sandwich" made the tracking opener. Mr. Beard brought in an idea which was totally perfect. Lightnin' Hopkins and his drummer, Spyder Kilpatrick, used to mesmerize the three of us with their nonchalant way of piecin' it together. And the best lesson learned? Bring yo'sef a paper-bagged snack in juke-joint fashion, put it on your floor-tom, have yo'sef a break with a Poke Chop Sandwich!

Another rough-cut special is the Robert Johnson-inspired "Hey Mr. Millionaire"—with a recording technique that matched the famed Johnson sessions. A performance in New York City found us backstage to say "hey" to Jeff Beck. (At the time of this writing, I can enjoyably mention that this friendship, which commenced with the year 1968, has remained a strong and valuable one.) In the dressing room, I asked, "Why don't you consider performing on our next record?" There was a brief, still silence, and I said, "I want you to sing."

He said, "But I don't sing."

I said, "That's the beauty of it. We'll do this à la Robert Johnson in a hotel room in Texas."

He said, "Fine. I'll book the show and we'll have a go," and the rest is history! We made a go of it, hotel room tradition, two blocks from the very building where Robert Johnson made his classic blues recordings in the 1930s. A handheld tape machine and two takes. One for the first verse and one for the second! Jeff can belt it out. Jeff's verbal performance singing on one of our favorites, "Hey Mr. Millionaire" . . . give that poor boy a dime!

For *XXX*, ZZ Top enlisted the handiness of another longstanding friend kept all these years. Mr. James Harmon dropped in with his Mississippi harmonica to lend his stellar talents on a few easy Triple X tracks. Pure juke joint. XXX served up some live sides too, for the fans taking the time to hang with th' boys. Got a mobile unit to follow us around to some small nightclubs—one in Hollywood, one in San Antonio, another in Austin, and one in Miami. The surprise-appearance club gigs. Plugged in and played. My personal pick: Dusty doin' "Teddy Bear" with Mr. Beard's cut-shuffle rhythm. So, so, sloooow.

We continued on our worldwide touring schedule. Some dates throughout Australia, then took the march over to New Zealand, then at the conclusion, the gear was to be transported by boat to England, our next engagement. This left us with about five months of holiday time. I remained as a newfound tourist in Auckland, made some wonderful new friends: Gavin Downey, Nicole Abbott, who took me 'round to Ponsby Road reggae clubs, the really late-night spots, gambling joints, and the specialty of the city . . . "The Mexican Cafe." No lie, it's there, right up the stair.

I came back to Hollywood and to H-town. Roots and rhythm. We booked the next series of recording sessions at Foam Box Recordings.

Mescalero (2003) . . .take it like ya like it, Mescalero Indians, Mescal, Mescaline . . . take it like ya' like it! The *Mescalero* tunes are like mixing papayas and mangos, chili and onions, rancheros and corridas, English and Spanish. The basics were reinvented. Here's another set of some fine tracks. The song "Mescalero" for starters! Remembering some time spent in Mexico City in the early '60s (Mexico City is a swell place), drove me straight away back to making another round of ZZ sound. The Spanish tune "Que Lastima" is a traditional Norteno tune and a toast found on any weekend in any crusty cantina. And the African-inspired instrumental "Crunchy." There's even another blues ballad, "Goin' So Good," drenched with pedal-steel guitar for a tear-jerking wail. The New Orleans-flavored "Punk Ass Boyfriend" got soul. Dusty offered up his best shoutin' vocal on "Piece," while another extreme eccentric from the South Texas lowlands jumped in with a colorful presence, talkin' 'bout one favorite ZZ theme, "Buck Nekkid." We all know 'bout 'dat! There's the shufflin' shuffle, "What It Is Kid?" . . . the one and only walkin' bass-line special . . . and probably the favorite from the set, "Alley-Gator," that fine chunk of change referring to our lil' Louisiana sweetie, AlleyCat. She's fine, fine, fine, and the song says it best: "She'll chew you up, that ain't no lie . . ." *Mescalero* is good.

Without question, the highlight of my professional career is standing up as Billy F Gibbons alongside my two best pals, Frank Beard and Dusty Hill, and having come into contact with some of the greatest artists and poets of the last century. These are the guys who set the stage for us to do what we do.

So, now you know. All the blues cats, all the great Texas experiences, influences from around this crazy world—too much to count, but all of it to remember!

BFG sez...

Quite the life, as they say . . .
done a lot . . .
WORKIN' ON DOIN' IT ALL
just good to be here.

Thanks for lettin' me tell
ya what this is all about.

As Lightnin' Hopkins said, *"The rubber on a wheel is faster than the rubber on a heel."*

THE CARS

THE PIVOTAL TURNING POINT IN THIS LIFELONG AFFAIR WITH CARS was the unpredicted appearance of **Houston's** sho-biz car dealer, **Art Grindle**, an eccentric kinda character advertising on the Saturday-morning TV program *Jungle Theater*. Here was this guy, stompin' and smashin' on car hoods, kickin' doors, puttin' a couple of mean dents on it, and then—right in the middle of one of **Tarzan's** vine-swingin' lion fights—announcing that the **Westheimer Road-Dog Special** was on! The first 10 viewers to arrive at the dealership put in $5 then drew numbers from a hat. The lucky winner got . . . **AG's Car of the Day.**

One fateful Saturday morning, my buddies and I—**Nickie Wiley** and **John Davidson**, **Chic Downs**, **Nicky Cobb**, and **Miguel Thompson**—arrived on time for the drawing. We tossed in a *peso* coin and drew our ticket. Lo and behold . . . lucky winner! Pay the front line! A **'54 Packard Golden Clipper**. Sawdust in the tranny, headlights stuck on high, painted from spray cans of *fake* gold mist . . . a real beater. But we threw caution out the window, piled in our newly acquired machine and headed straight for the **Mexican border**. This "winner" of an automobile—we called it **"the Pack"**—became the all-around, pass-around car. Despite the rear-end howlin', oil drippin', bad steerin', obnoxious upholstery, bad brakes, rusted-out beer-can floorboard holes, whoever needed the keys, of course, just picked 'em up, fired it up, and rolled. It ran forever.

Needless to say, we survived the Pack, but, as **Lightnin' Hopkins** said, "The rubber on a wheel is faster than the rubber on a heel." Instant realization that cars and guitars was where it was at. But what made 'em faster than you and me? Hot-roddin'.

After returning from **Mexico City** in the early '60s, first guitar in hand, I went to see **Dick Axell**, just setting up shop in **Texas**. Out from **California**, he had torched and restyled his **'60s T-Bird "Desafinado"** into one of the 10 Best Customs of the early '60s. His sidekick, **Redhead Fred**, was the in-th'-house, do-anything body man, panel-beater, top-chopper, pinstriper . . . so, I got over to there and had Redhead Fred's stripin' brush lay lines on that guitar of mine, and brought custom car hot-roddin' into the land of the electric.

And now, as this "gettin' a band thing together" shaped up, we needed a car . . . **a band car** . . . Yo! Got a super-simple anonymobile, a **'64 Dardge Dot**—sand-tan, two-door, three-on-the-tree, no radio, no air-conditionin', no heater, no prob. We rolled. It was band wagon, taco wagon, tequila wagon, make-out wagon, you name it . . . it was there, waitin' to do it all. And this car was something to shout about! We hit the frontera, braggin' on these over-the-road ZZ escapades . . . *everything* goin' down out there. We drove that car places where Jeeps feared to tread. Drove the livin'

The '72 scene with Stevie P. and Kenny C. "Francene," you know what I mean! Dig the Caddie.

daylights out of it, and diggin' it all the while! It was the ride. The **"Manic Mechanic."** Yep, that's the one. Listen to the song's first few bars . . . it's the one . . . the *Band Car*.

STREET RACING DELUXE 'N' KUSTOM KINGS

Into the street . . . **GTOs, Chevelles, big-block Camaros, Hemi-fied Mopars**. They ruled the street-racing road. Takin' a bet on a moment's notice. Out on **Highway 6**, same place where **"Master of Sparks"** took place, we and all the outlaw runners were gunnin' for "pink slips" . . . who gonna get there fastest and get there first!? Hit the starting line and hit the finish line, sistuh! "Fast" is a bet, and faster is better.

It was Rock 'n' Roll shootouts, battles of the bands, after-hours hangouts, and open-range runnin' and super-powered drag racing. Hands-on wrenching, technical tamperin', it all goes back to the '20s, workin' thru the '30s, '40s, '50s, '60s, and on . . . ain't no end in sight for the *need for speed*. Serious business.

Meanwhile, the whole kustom kar thing was goin' on, and without question, the innovators—**Harry Westergard, George and Sam Barris, Ed "Big Daddy" Roth, Daryl Starbird, Dean Jeffries, Gene Winfield, Gene Watson, Dick Dean, Von Dutch**, monster-shirter **Stanley Mouse, Pete Chapouris** and **Jake Jacobs, Chuck Lombardo Sr.** and **Jr**. at California Street Rods, hot-rod visionary **Robert Williams, Roy Brizio**—great customizers and artists, redesigning, shaping, styling. They were inventing car art pop magnetism. No rules, no holds barred. Art forms yet to be classified. And the high-stylin', high profilin' traditions continue today—**Cole Foster, Jimmy Shine, Gary Howard, Rudy Rodriguez, Rumble Rodders, Shifters, Pedestrian Killers, Burbank Choppers, Throttlers, Kontinentals**, all the hammer kings . . . *Chrome, Smoke, and Bar-B-Q*.

I started a first-shot custom with two guys down in the Houston hot-rod scene. **G-man Barret** and (the return of the great pinstriper) **Redhead Fred** . . . one mo' time! On a primered 1951 Shoebox Ford, we went about chopping five inches out of the headline, lowering the car cig-pack height, frenching and molding in the mandatory DeSoto toothed grille, frenching the head lights, frenching the taillights, and sho' 'nuff, making the obligatory trip to **Tijuana** to get that famous TJ tuck 'n' roll interior. That car was the first real custom I did. We got it runnin' and rollin' 'round '72 . . . got it rockin', too.

Lean, clean, haulin' hay, and ready to play!

THE KUSTOM KAR VISIONARIES
were inventing car art pop magnetism.
NO RULES, NO HOLDS BARRED.
Art forms yet to be classified.

The early boys… Texas brush…
just lookin' for some Tush!

ELIMINATOR COUPE

E Coupe time. Around 1976, I ran into **Pete Chapouris** and **Jake Jacobs**, the two cool cats runnin' **Pete and Jake's Hot Rod Repair**. Both their '34 coupes branded the attitude of pure, Holy-Hell hot rod. After some gearhead *tête à tête*, we chased down a primo '33 three-window and set about starting about what we wanted . . . just a hot rod!

Pete and **Jake** kindly turned me on to **Don Thelen**'s whack shack, **Buffalo Motor Cars** over in **Paramount**. The expert shop-choppers there, **Ron Jones** and **Birdman**, took the first task at hand, makin' that initial cut through the top. Ain't no turnin' back now. As the old saying goes, "Anyone can put one back together, but it takes a real man to cut one up." Sing it, brother!

I got down to work with some really sharp operators—superb automotive stylist **Larry Wood** and artist deluxe **Kenny Youngblood**, who laid the impressive **ZZ** lines across the side panels of the coupe. There remained the dilemma dealing with the "correct" imaging of the double-Z design, driver's side and passenger side. The passenger side **ZZ** was backward . . . reversed . . . so Mr. Youngblood said, "Just drive past shiny windows, you'll see the **Z** any side you wanna be on!" Go figure!

I made a lot of friends and hot-rod *fiends*, a tight clan of rod builders—**Dan Fink** at **DF Metal Works**, **Thelen** at **Buffalo**, and, of course, **Pete** and **Jake**, fabricated the chassis for the lil' red '33. The fine folks at **Holly Carburetor**, **Wall Pantera**, who fab'd the rims, **Art Chrisman Engines**, **Vic Edelbrock**'s specialty outfit, **Steve Zeiber** at **American Racing Wheels**, **Vic Kitchens**, the great interior man, and the enigmatic **Zoomer**, whose wiring job kept the car from burnin' up . . . a fine assembly of best of the best.

After five long years of real, hands-on hard work, hammerin' down with metalsmiths and engine specialists, and stunning squirters of candied paint, the **Eliminator Coupe**—artistically complete, top to bottom, side to side, repowered, repainted, loads of "go fast"—was seeing light at the end of a long tunnel. It was Hot Rod.

After the wait, the curtain lifted for the unveiling of the lil' red coupe, which ultimately graced the cover of **ZZ Top's** *Eliminator* album. Coast to coast, border to border, the **Eliminator Coupe** was everywhere, burnin' rubber into this new world called **MTV**, showing up on screen with the release of **"Gimme All Your Lovin'," "Sharp Dressed Man,"** and **"Legs."**

30

65

65 Covers "Jet Pro... acteristics"—"Dy-
namometers"—"R... Pipes"—"Speed
95 Tuning"—Porting— ALL MAKES OF
CARS. Authentic— Equipment—Get
50 up to ten more W...

35 **SAV...**

71 Get racing speed...
creases from any...
95 Build fast Stock...
Get construction...
95 Economy secrets...
'California Auto...
est ideas). Conve...
8 "1951 Speed Equi... FIVE ITEMS
ing," and "Water... ostpaid

SPEED — POWER

NEWHOUSE AUTOMOTIVE INDUSTRIES

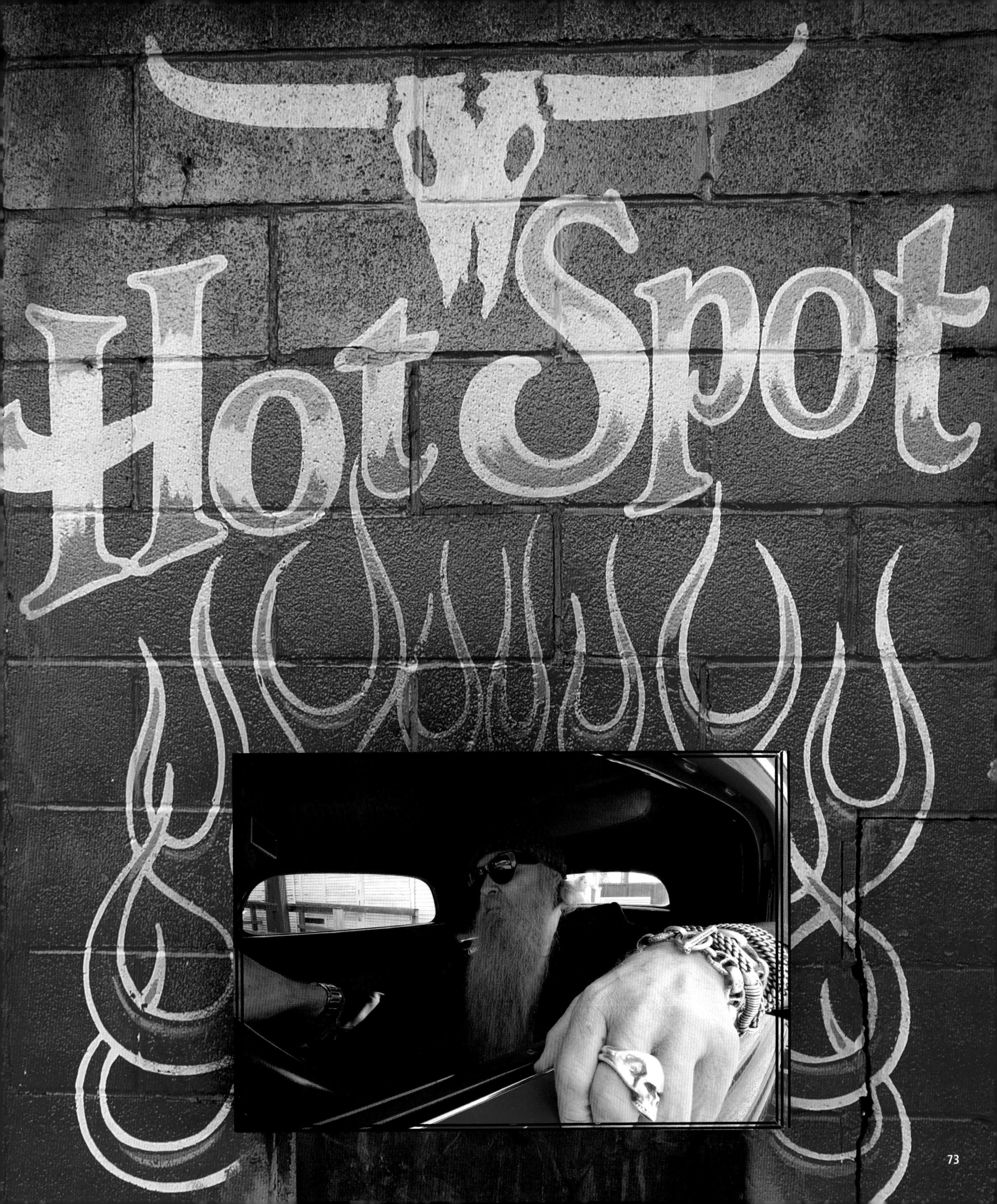
Hot Spot

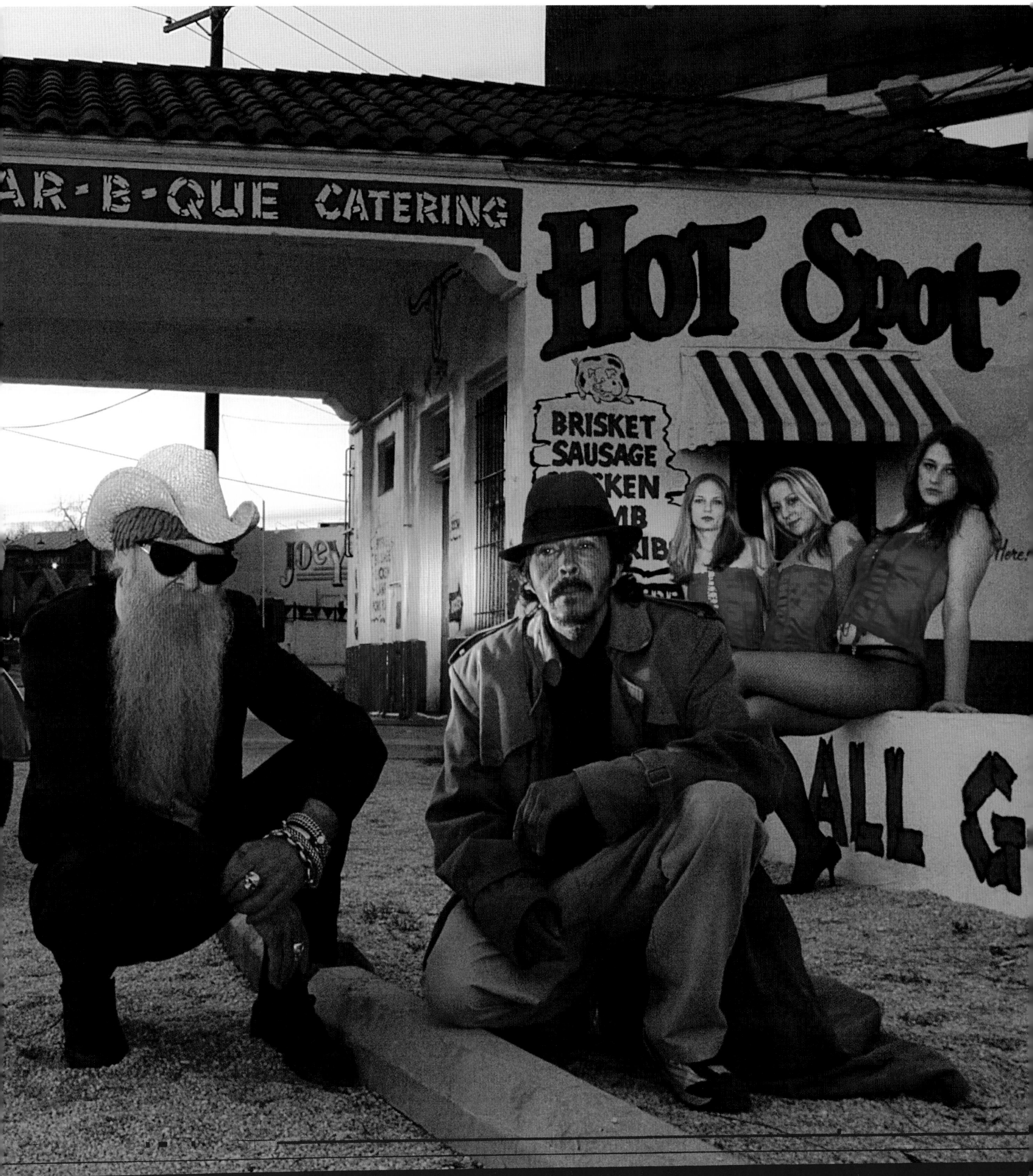
AR-B-QUE CATERING
HOT Spot
BRISKET
SAUSAGE

LEAPIN' LIMO

The *Afterburner* album appeared, and suddenly **Leapin' Limo**—a stretched **'48 Pontiac Silver Streak**—screamed through the **"Velcro Fly"** video.

This rusting hulk was discovered and lifted out of the back 40 of a Texas ranch with the assistance of my car-guitar freak friend, **Jimmy Emerson**. The car seemed a prime candidate for the usual chop-shop make-ready. So, after a bit of brainstorming, we sent it over to **California Street Rods** in **Huntington Beach** under the watchful eyes of **Chuck Lombardo Sr.** and **Jr.**

Buzz-saw master **Dick Dean** stretched the car 40 awesome inches and chopped the roof lowdown 4 1/2 inches. With a big-block powertrain knockin' under hood and a splash of **"ZZ"** down the sides, this one was definitely "fly" and named with the help of American Racing Wheels. The car swooped up **Paula Abdul**, and she showed the bearded boys how to shake the groove. Now anything goes! Let's **Velcro Fly** and "Leap"!

CADZZILLA

At the evening conclusion of one particularly long and lengthy road run, there was a way-borracho'd meeting on the **Mexican border** with Cadillac stylist **Mr. Larry Erickson**, heading up **Cadillac's** design studio. Larry, myself, and hot rodder **Jack Chisenhall** attempted to answer the question "What'cha gonna hot-rod now?"

So, after a flash and furious exchange of the notorious bar napkin, an image emerged to answer "What's next?" A vision of elegance, something with length, something with gracefulness, to go hand-in-hand with the success of the **Eliminator Coupe**. Crawlin' from the wreckage of the late-night revelry in that infamous cantina, our bar-napkin **'48 Cad** was fixed, tricked, and transformed . . . here came **CadZZilla!**

Both rod *and* custom—this was the extreme. Encouraged by *Hot Rod Magazine* and *Harley-Davidson Motorcycles,* the gauntlet was laid on the table to complete this work of elegance and meet an unreal deadline. The heat was on—raw steel to be reshaped and completed in 180 days. But, somehow, at the close of six months, the key was in the ignition and **CadZZilla** fired up. We had succeeded in the impossible. With the enthusiasm of the great body man **Craig Naff**, and the staff at **Coddington's** outfit, out rolled the unbelievable streamlined mass.

It was stretched, it was slammed, taking on a personality that indeed remains timelessly beautific. The profile was purely organic and orgasmic. Beautiful . . . and a monstrously strong runner, going where you wanted it to go, on time and in style. From the demonic **Bonneville Mooneyes** tank up front in the grille, only a simple chrome sphere profiles the sectioned hood and B pillar, up to the stretched Art Deco roofline. The **Cadillac** theme of bumper bullets runs from the grille, through the side-mirrors, even to the steering wheel. It's hot rod and radical custom, from the ground up. **CadZZilla** gots everythang!

from mild...

to wild

Mi tierra cafe

FIXED

TRICKED

TRANSFORMED

HOGZZILLA

Halfway through the construction of **CadZZilla**, **Larry Erickson** envisioned a complement to escort **CadZZilla** in proper fashion. I had the good fortune to bump into the **Harley-Davidson** crew in the Minneapolis airport, coming and going. We made a date and planned a project to create these **HogZZilla** bikes, built around the latest and greatest design in the Harley line.

Delivered to **SO-CAL Speed Shop's** head honcho, **Pedro 'C'**, the resulting refabrication turned out not one, but two gnarly Harleys to escort **CadZZilla**.

Executed in 58 days. The custom panels and detailing treatment were in exact style of **CadZZilla**—fender panels, side trims, all matched. Nicknamed **"HogZZilla 1"** and **"HogZZilla 2"** . . . modified to the max. Yes. The EVO pair served well doing what they were intended to do: accompany **CadZZilla** to every occasion. **HogZZilla 1** and **2** led the grand entry parade with **Willy G.** and **Mrs. Willy Davidson**, and **Billy and Karen Davidson** at Daytona **Bike Week '92**.

MAMBO COUPE

A chopped **'36** found in a shop, nearly ready for the road. But **John Bolin** and I were talkin' *guitars* when out of the blue, I think just to mess with his mind, I said, "Oh yeah, I need a **'36 three-window coupe**, too."

He replied in a beat, saying, "All steel, of course, but would you prefer a stocker or would you like it chopped?"

I said that I like 'em low and slow, and he said, "I got just what you want."

Keepin' in mind, **Bolin's** one of those enigmatic characters who can do anything ya want . . . find it, build it, you got it! So we immediately headed out to meet up at a garage maybe two blocks from his shop in Boise, Idaho! And sure enough, there it stood, black, shiny, and whacked to the max. I cut a deal with a promise to see it through, and off we went, straight to **SO-CAL Speed Shop**, where it got the once-over and make-ready for rockin' th' road.

We found a box of Australian **Mambo surf shirts** in the boot, and thought, "Well, it's gotta have a name," so, **"Mambo"** it was.

First touch. I was on a break from the studio back in **L.A.**, workin' up some designs for some new stage wardrobing—bracelets, chains, skulls—with **Ryk Maverick**. We had cast a skeleton head for his showroom, which was quickly spotted by the **SO-CAL** guys, who took our request to weld it into the grille . . . chewin' its way out. It looked pretty wicked, torch marks and all. The sinister appeal was a no-brainer. This was around '94.

Next, the interior. It was needin' somethin' . . . but what? Indeed, **Pete Chapouris** had stashed in a storeroom a well-worn, red-leather sofa that he grew up with. and he had the presence of mind to send the hide to cover the seats with. Period-perfect patina. The hammerhead's hood got punch 'n' stamp louvering, and a wheel and tire change laid the stance just right. **Mambo** hit the streets runnin'. Sweet.

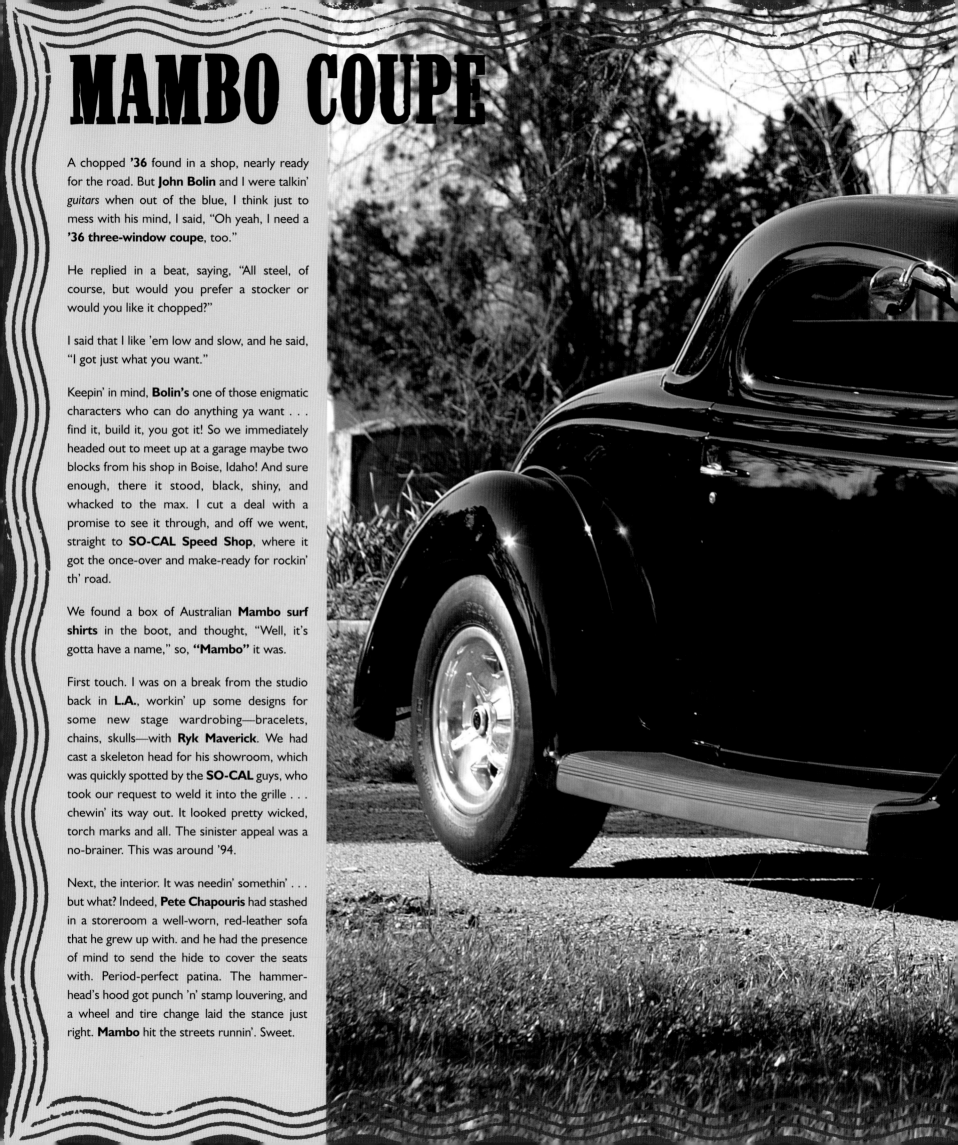

KOPPERHED

So, now, what about the **Ford coupe** just settin' out back of the **SO-CAL** garage? A fine rendering lying on the drafting table of car artist **Steve Stanford** set the wheels in motion. Three-window coupes disappeared after the **'30s**, but the lines of the '50 lent a phantom treatment possibility, as if it could have had rolled out of the factory itself.

Kopperhed commenced. The welding rods were lit and the torch-work began. A tremendous amount of restructuring and restyling was now bringing to life something that was conceivably assembly-line structured. The roof was chopped 3 inches, panels were beat, doors were extended 10 inches, and, along with a lot of imagination, sweat, and work, somethin' cool came 'round. We started on it in '95, and it took over a year of slicin' and dicin' to design and customize. Pure **Ford,** thru and thru, from the **'57 T-Bird Tri-Power V-8** down to genny hubcaps and baby rings, it's real.

JB Donaldson recast a rare **'50** deluxe steering wheel, blendin' in with some NOS copper fabric found in a warehouse for the inside. **Kopperhed**, a radically restyled custom was the deceiving one. Yeah, the three-window that "never was," but it's got that certain, "I drove it in high school" kinda vibe. The essence of cruisin'.

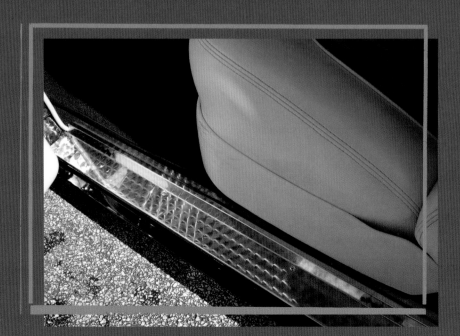

PETE CHAPOURIS

Pete Chapouris is head honcho of SO-CAL Speed Shop and founding partner of Pete and Jake's Hot Rod Repair. A California original who has been hot rodding and customizing since forever, Pete has worked with Billy to build and create many of his famous cars.

I first met up with Billy at a hot rod show in North Carolina in 1976. I'm at this event, hanging in the parking lot waiting for my partner Jake to come out. Next thing I know, Billy Gibbons comes walking out of a field with a girl on each arm! He comes over and puts his sunglasses halfway down his nose and gives me a look and asks, "Are you from Pete and Jake's?" He told me he'd sent me the latest ZZ Top album with a note attached. I told him I received the album, but there was no note with it, so I just assumed a buddy of mine had dropped it off.

He asked how much longer we were gonna be in town, and I said two more days. He said he had a couple of days off 'coz they just played Knoxville. So he offered to come over tomorrow, and I was like, "Yeah, sure," but I didn't really expect him to show up 'coz you hear that a lot.

So bright and early the next morning, Billy shows up and we spent the entire day together. He was talking about a car he wanted to build, which later turned into the Eliminator. Now that I know him, I'm sure he was on the band bus doing drawings of how he wanted it to look. I mean he had all these magazines, he had really done his homework.

About a year later, he came out to the L.A. Roadster Show and he was going to buy a car, but there was nothing around that was any good. I told him, "Billy, you're going about this in the wrong direction." I said, "Take the money that you've got and let's just go out and find a nice three-window coupe. We'll work with Don Thelen and we'll get the chassis up so that it's a roller and Don can do the bodywork, chop the top, clean up the body, and paint it." It was the last turnkey chassis we did out of Pete and Jake's, and that became the Eliminator car. It took about two and a half to three years to get it finished. It started in '78 and we were done by '81.

The only thing that changed from the original concept was we were gonna put different wheels and rims on it. Other than that, nothing changed. That was our first outing with him, and every year since we've done something together. We'll build a car or a bike. It might just be him coming over and hanging out.

CadZZilla was next and he did that with Boyd Coddington. I had sold my business at that time. I was working for another company, but I went over to Boyd's

every Thursday afternoon to look at their progress. I was really jealous cause I didn't get to work on it.

Later on, I left my desk job and opened a place up in Crestline, California, and did another car for him, a '36 black three-window coupe. Then he got the idea with Larry Davidson to build two matching bikes that would accompany CadZZilla in a parade. They would be like parade bikes. We did about half a dozen motorcycles including those parade bikes, now named HogZZilla, as well as some street bikes.

Those bikes were major stuff. We debuted those at Daytona and no one had ever heard of us in the bike world, and they were blown away that hot rodders would build those kinds of motorcycles. It actually changed the whole styling of motorcycles from the last 15 years. No one had ever done a full-fender bike and made it look right. Larry Erickson's design was dead on the money.

After that we did a '50 Ford called Kopperhed. That car was designed by Billy and Steve Stanford. We made that car a reality. I had a lot of stuff going with him at that time, early1990s, 1990-95. There was five years in there that we did a lot of activity.

We also did a '68 Cadillac convertible for him, a black one that was nicely lowered. Now we're working on a cream-colored '82 El Camino for him. We've chopped it, and we're doing our deal on it. We've also got a '61 Caddy and a '32 roadster built by Rudy Rodriguez, and we're giving it sort of a shave and a haircut--a hood, redo the interior, do the wheels and tires--so it's got Billy's look on it.

He's got extremely good taste, some of it's off the wall, but 90 percent of what he brings you is doable. He has a realistic look on the things that he does from a driver's standpoint. Billy is a really good artist. We can talk and he can sketch these ideas out, and it's like working with a professional artist. The guy is really good!

Also, he is extremely intelligent and very, very savvy. When he doesn't know something, he doesn't bullshit his way into it, he asks. Billy is not a know-it-all. Working with him is really fun. We work over the phone and with faxes, and it's awesome.

I think Gibbons is so contrary to his appearance. If people are meeting him for the first time and they spend five minutes with the guy they're blown away by his intelligence. It's sort of diametrically opposed to his image. He researches stuff where he makes a conscious decision of what he wants to do, and then he figures out how to go about doing it. That's one of the things I like so much about him.

Another thing, in talking with guys like Eric Clapton, Billy has been true to his sound. He's professed to be one of the best blues guitar players in the world, and I believe it. I've been with him and watched him jam, and he's just incredible. I mean he's an incredible person, an incredible creative being that has such varied interests, but somehow they all dovetail into making him the unique character he is.

He's generous and kind to a fault. Not to the point where he's a pushover. I mean if something's not going right, or the way he wants it, he'll let you know, but never in an unkind or disrespectful way. I can't say enough about the guy!

SLAMPALA

Slampala . . . a **1962 Chevrolet Super Sport**. This one came after Kopperhed, in '97-'98. I picked it up from another hot-rod buddy, **Del Ushenko**, a rod man with a keen eye for solid straight ones. One evening, while traveling aboard the band bus way up West, we were fuelin' up at a truck stop, and I grabbed a copy of an auto-trading magazine just to have a late-night, groovy read. Because of its low stance, the Chev pictured looked like a misprint, or maybe a ready-to-go custom.

It was curious enough to tweak our interest and, sure enough, Del's voice at the other end of the line spoke pure hot rod! I knew I was engaged with someone knowing the business, and this car was all business! Del scored it through an estate, a real runner with just a few miles on it.

Again, with some bad-ass detailing from our favorite spec-tech wizards over at **SO-CAL** and **California Street Rods**, it was asphalt-hungry in quick time. A simple, original stocker—with the exception of **Air Ride Technology suspension**—it's a hop-up, hop-down affair. Lower is better . . . this one is no exception!

Original paint and body with some slight mods to the interior, especially the **'60 Impala** boomerang wheel and matched dash knobs, recast in Phoenix, Arizona, from 1960 originals. Thank you **Mr. Donaldson**! This low-slung roller is one of the daily drivers, ready to prowl **the Strip** in style.

ALL NEW!

A HOP-UP HOP-DOWN AFFAIR

325ı CUSTOM

What!? A custom **BMW?!** **"8 Ball B."** Now, what you gonna do?

Well, under the thoughtful design talents of our favorite hot-rod shop, let's start with some lowering, some big wheel/big rim and monster rubber, some punch 'n' stamp hood louvers . . . put the ride forward, man! Hip-hop, over-the-top Euro ride. Add the **8 Ball** all over it. Put 'em on the gear stick, put 'em on the wheels, nail 'em all around the thing and soup it up—spunk and stealth deluxe. Top up, or top down, you gonna get to **Antonio's Friday afternoon tamales,**

ets of
better
manu-
been
equip

ALON

Co.

m
T
s M
M
f
h
f
a
f o
o t f
a igni
T

Jr
wi
26

CADILLAC '61

As customizers loosened their strict recognition of particular years, later-model automobiles became more fashionable. These days, almost anything goes.

The "Toast of The Town" is the rad-bad, '61 Cad... elegant bubbletop Coupe DeVille from GM... layin' low with no particular place to go. The only modification necessary was the lowering treatment. This car can lay frame and sit, huggin' the ground with Space-Age thinness and clean looks. It's daggerish, dangerous and an example of what dependability's all about, ready for Tuxedo Town. Get behind the wheel and haul L.A. to New York City.

DANGEROUS

DAGGERISHLY

'32 HIGHBOY ROADSTER

Now then, the **"Deuce,"** the real hot rod. The most elegant addition to this collection is the *coup de grace*, a real-steel **'32 Ford roadster**. Just like you woulda seen in '47. Pulled out of a barn, put together, and freshened up by **Rudy Rodriguez** at **Fullerton Fabrications**, this one's a true-blue, red-light runnin' **highboy**. Powered with a rare **French**-built **V-8 flathead**, hopped up, and outfitted with some dredged-up '40s pawn-shop, back-alley, swap-meet speed stuff, it's a real show-stopper. The essence of roddin'. **No-Lo axle**, '44 dashboard, '39 banjo wheel, **LaSalle** tranny, '39 taillights—all good. Get yo' girl . . . *shift* and roll.

COUP DE GRACE

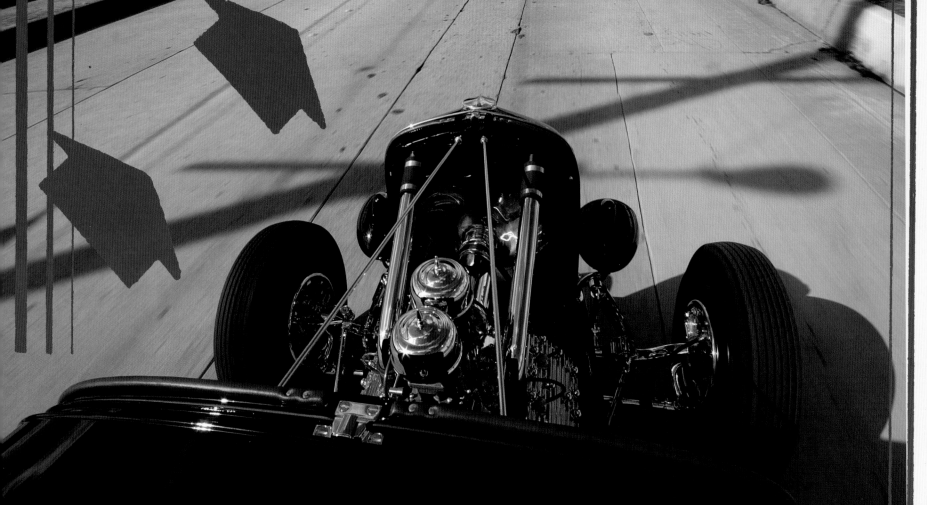

BFG sez...
man, what a plan ...
CARS AND GUITARS.
Do it to it!

I liked the words of Muddy Waters, recounted by Keith Richards: **"You don't have to be the best one, just be a good 'un."**

THE GUI

CARS AND GUITARS . . . DOIN' IT FO' ME . . . YEAH, CARS, GUITARS, SOLID ROCK.

Big-scene surfing, with an eye on them electrics.

The electric became the driving force in all the great records heard on the radio and on the record player. Without question, seein' Elvis Presley in Houston affected me the way it affected just about everyone else . . . rebellious and strong, and I personally equated that with electric guitar! It was loud! Raucous and powerful! The new tool of the trade, I guess. Gunslinger material.

Everyday I'm a lucky man. Electrics only—anything else is bad luck. The electric made small combos make sounds dynamic and bigger than life, certainly bigger than giant horn sections. They distorted harmonics that filled big square rooms or small square rooms. Not round-room sounds, these were harsh, powerful sounds and, in hand, it is undeniable . . . it's seriously strong.

When I was a kid back in H-town there was a four-piece combo, The VanTels, that played up the street. I could hear 'em good. I became friends with the brothers who were the guitarists. They built hot-rod cars, all the cool stuff—chopped and lowered '57 Chevy coupes, a chopped T roadster. Real wicked. And they played really good on all the right gears. A red '61 Les Paul pinstriped by Von Dutch (!), an original '58 Fender Jazzmaster (the rare one), gold-sparkle drums, the works. And when they made a record, that pretty much did me in. I thought, "If they can do it, then this is where I wanna go."

Meanwhile, me and my buddy pretty much holed up with the guitar and set about learning from records, 78s, 45 RPM vinyl records, whatever, man. I learned what I was hearing, and I began liking what I was playing. Self-taught. Just wanted three chords that I kept hearing, and that was all, those first three chords.

Spring of 1965-66, I became acquainted with Dale Velzy, one of the early West Coast surfboard builders, the same Dale Velzy that Velzyland, the Hawaiian surf spot, is named after. The surf scene, believe it or not, also had a big impact on guitar. In those early days, the guitar's image shot up and, at the same time, sometime in the '50s, guys like Velzy started shaping boards in SoCal. His boards, all long and all wood, hit the West Coast. Slab board for guitar and slab board for the surf. Gotta have it! And Mr. Velzy had hotwired it from way deep in his soul.

What I liked about Dale was he built and drove a "windowless" deuce coupe. If he wasn't knee-deep in the fiberglass yard, shaping boards, he was in the saltwater, and he knew how to get there and get there fast! I believe Dale was the first one hittin' the beach in a supercharged, steel deuce, surfboard hangin' out the back window! A good thing, 'coz after a day in the water, he had to fly back to his shop and shape for the waiting customers who wanted the best.

Young Willy G. with Willie Dixon.

With respect to Bo, the show gotta go!

I had a giant fixation, though, on hot rod cars and I was playing enough guitar to get in trouble. Dale found that to be rather entertaining. It was much to his liking, and our mutual interests have remained longstanding. When I went back to California in 1985, I saw him after 20 years or so, and we still maintained our pact! His son, Matt, a great guy, who lives back in Hawaii, confirms all the tall tales. It's all there. Cars, guitars, and everything else.

So, on to SoCal . . . Huntington Beach, Rincon, San Onofre, was breaking. The West Coast mystery men, Fender and Velzy, were shapin' it up, makin' music and makin' waves. On one hand, you had the Blues guys doin' their thing, and then you had this West Coast/Texas combination taking on this new contraption called "electric guitar." From The Ventures to Howlin' Wolf, from Dick Dale to B. B. King, that whole guitar/surf/Blues hookup. . . Euphoria. Anyway, we were learnin' from Laguna Beach, up north to Malibu, back down to Texas and Mississippi. A whirlwind of input!

SOLOING

Now, check it out—the guitar solo. The lead guitarist was emerging from the puzzle. And just the right piece to the puzzle. The early rockin' soloists . . . Scotty Moore, Chuck Berry, Bo Diddley, Buddy Holly, Speedy West, Jimmy Bryant, Buddy Guy, Grady Martin, Luther Tucker, Freddie Roulette, Mr. Steve "Inventor of Soul Guitar" Cropper, Jimmie (James Brown) Nolan.

Fast forward to Keith, Steve Vai, Satriani, Peter Green, Mick Taylor, Eddie Van Halen, Jeff Beck . . . all these great players taking soloing style to the outer limits, putting the solo in a spotlight position on the deck. Being stimulated by guys like that is like peeling the onion, as the old saying goes . . . gets sweeter with each layer. Learn how to play what you wanna to hear. A simple statement maybe, but now—with volume, tone, outboard effects, devices, a lot of woodsheddin', and a lot of blind luck—the solo guitar is on.

Blues shredders and metal-headers alike can take the guitar from chunky rhythms and hammer steel balls into silver dollars. Solo . . . So-Low! The nighttime is the right time to view the bending, twisting, and squeezing out the juice. Certainly, the solo is an essence of cool guitar . . . as it should be.

DESIGN

I credit Bo Diddley, with his gifted sense of design and applied skills, as well as a few select visionary draftsmen, with opening the doorway to many different guitar shapes. Keep in mind, most manufacturers of electric guitars in the '50s and '60s (and even on into the present) rarely considered fabricating special, one-off designs.

One exception was the arrangement Bo Diddley had with Gretsch Guitars. They custom-built many of his designs, including his square guitar, Big B. During the recent ZZ Top recordings, the engineering crew and I snaked through the guitar vault searching for that "certain-something" guitar . . . and there was Bo's old Jupiter Thunderbird!

We wouldn't risk subjecting such a rare instrument to the rigors of the road, so a new model was re-created with some BFG Mojo thrown in for good measure. It's become the main stage guitar with a groove, and the "Billy-Bo" Jupiter Thunderbird is now in production with Fender and Gretsch, an uncompromising example of radical movement in the design arena. Pure shapes of Rock 'n' Roll, very nasty pieces of pure Rock 'n' Roll.

Good design—great design—maintains the designer's sometimes peculiar visions without disturbing sound or tone. Instruments that stand up to the range and variety of great pop icons . . . the electric guitar. Witness some of these great stylists . . . B. B. King, Albert King, John Mayer, Carlos Santana, and lot of fellow Texas musicians, guys like Jimmie Vaughan, Stevie Ray, Van Wilx, Eric Johnson, Joe Ely, Ronnie Earl, Kid Ramos, Dave Gonzales, Gatemouth Brown, and T-Bone Walker . . . add 'em to the mix and sail on. Listeners will know who that guitar player is. Recognize the STYLE? The TONE?

The CRUSH?

It's in the hands, brah. Not necessarily dependent on any particular guitar or any particular amp. It's what you do with the hands. I've seen junker solid bodies transformed into solid-body gems, thanks to the grip of the hands. Just do it with the hands . . . no worries 'bout guitars or amps, just take care o' th' hands . . .

I too, picked up whatever I could along the way. There's nothing more enjoyable than pickin' up a geetar and bangin' it, findin' th' best frets, findin' those sounds. The bottom line is love what you do, chase what you wanna hear! I personally choose to use everything available as far as the hands go. And what goes on in the head—what goes on in my head can be quite overwhelming—count on using everything you can! Get meaner, faster, quicker . . . "You don't have to be the best one, just be a good 'un."

COLLECTING

When Jimi Hendrix and I became friends, what he was dreaming up went far beyond what the electric guitar was designed to do! He took the instrument to other lofty, psychedelic, undefined realms, and moments that musicians count as inspirational. But I started checkin' out different guitars. My friend and associate, Red "Tighten Up" Pharoah, started talking guitars with me. He was the guy with Archie Bell and the Drells, the "Tighten Up" guys. Red is a diehard Fender player. He rang up one afternoon to let me know that he had an instrument. Not a Les Paul, but it had humbucking pickups on it. We cut a deal and the instrument he offered turned out to be a 1958 Gibson Flying V! Yeah, you right! The "V," respected as not only rarities, but as terrific tone machines as well.

Before "vintage," it was quite common to go down and pick up a Fender Strat, Tele, Esquire, whatever was hanging in the pawn shop, drag it out for the weekend, and turn it in after th' gig. Cash out on Friday, trash it out on Saturday, praise it on Sunday, and cash it back in on Monday. Not too much regard was placed on any particular instrument at that time, we just went down and grabbed somethin' to hammer on. However, after seeing Eric Clapton playing his 'Burst and Marshall amp in '68, I began the search to acquire one of my own.

There were a few of them out there, but they were rare. They were sought after because of the humbucking pickup, invented in 1955 by Seth Lover, a designer with Gibson, and first produced in 1957. The old single-coil pickup had been developed with great success, but was prone to hum, hiss, and scratch . . . quite noisy and irritating. Seth Lover determined that by taking two single-coil pickups and combining them together with reverse polarity, they cancelled out the strange frequencies and you got pure, clean tone.

At Kurt's early vintage showroom. Take note of the welcome sign and the mirrored Cadillac reflection.

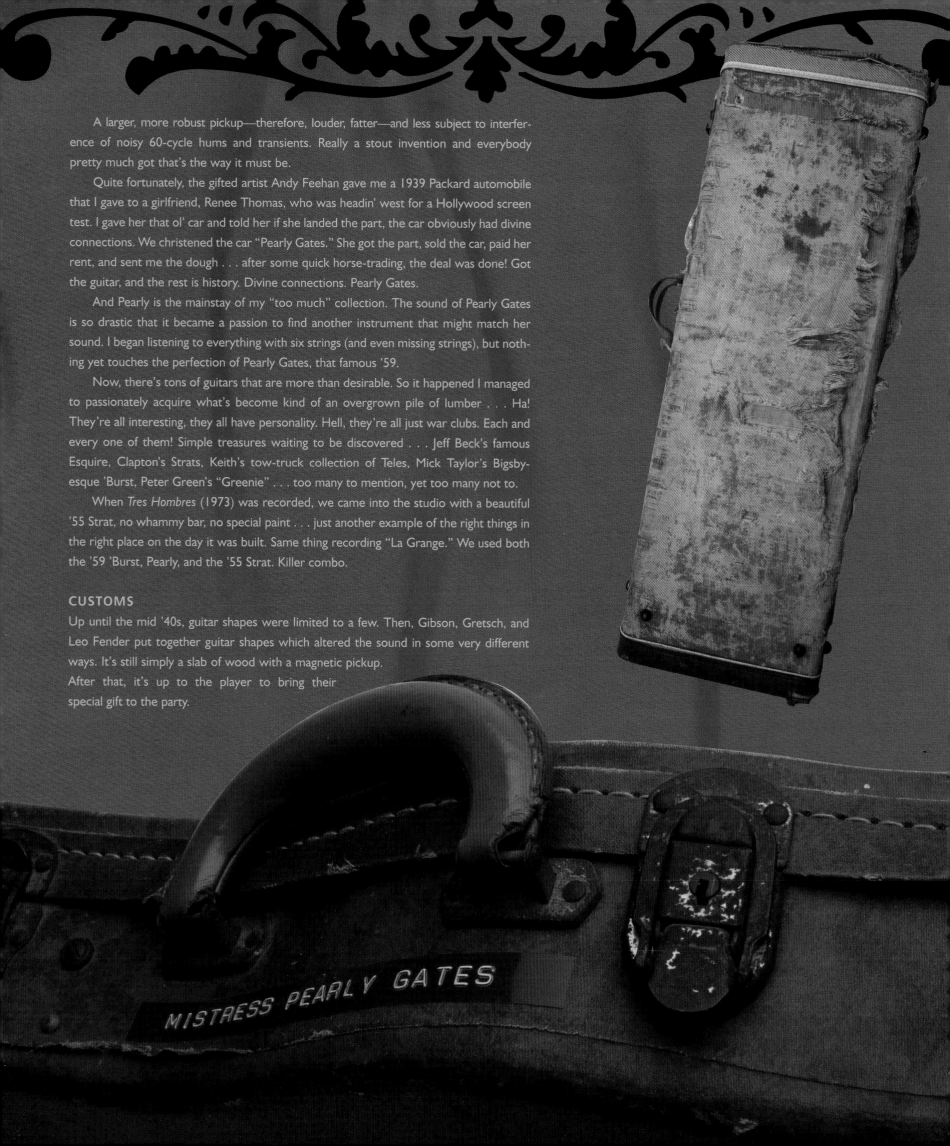

A larger, more robust pickup—therefore, louder, fatter—and less subject to interference of noisy 60-cycle hums and transients. Really a stout invention and everybody pretty much got that's the way it must be.

Quite fortunately, the gifted artist Andy Feehan gave me a 1939 Packard automobile that I gave to a girlfriend, Renee Thomas, who was headin' west for a Hollywood screen test. I gave her that ol' car and told her if she landed the part, the car obviously had divine connections. We christened the car "Pearly Gates." She got the part, sold the car, paid her rent, and sent me the dough . . . after some quick horse-trading, the deal was done! Got the guitar, and the rest is history. Divine connections. Pearly Gates.

And Pearly is the mainstay of my "too much" collection. The sound of Pearly Gates is so drastic that it became a passion to find another instrument that might match her sound. I began listening to everything with six strings (and even missing strings), but nothing yet touches the perfection of Pearly Gates, that famous '59.

Now, there's tons of guitars that are more than desirable. So it happened I managed to passionately acquire what's become kind of an overgrown pile of lumber . . . Ha! They're all interesting, they all have personality. Hell, they're all just war clubs. Each and every one of them! Simple treasures waiting to be discovered . . . Jeff Beck's famous Esquire, Clapton's Strats, Keith's tow-truck collection of Teles, Mick Taylor's Bigsbyesque 'Burst, Peter Green's "Greenie" . . . too many to mention, yet too many not to.

When *Tres Hombres* (1973) was recorded, we came into the studio with a beautiful '55 Strat, no whammy bar, no special paint . . . just another example of the right things in the right place on the day it was built. Same thing recording "La Grange." We used both the '59 'Burst, Pearly, and the '55 Strat. Killer combo.

CUSTOMS

Up until the mid '40s, guitar shapes were limited to a few. Then, Gibson, Gretsch, and Leo Fender put together guitar shapes which altered the sound in some very different ways. It's still simply a slab of wood with a magnetic pickup.
After that, it's up to the player to bring their special gift to the party.

MISTRESS PEARLY GATES

Dig them flashy fluorescent geetars.

Anyway, I got more and more into design study and set up a proper drafting board, producing prototypes, all shapes, all sizes, which affected the sound. Different shapes, different sound.

Something all great guitarists seem to agree on is that an aesthetically pleasing shape will most likely produce an aesthetically pleasing sound. Yet, there is no guarantee that this instrument or that can be predictably evaluated before completion—it's always an after-the-fact game. My first custom commission was in 1972 with George Gruhn Guitars in Nashville. His backroom shop was run by Tut Taylor and Randy Wood. Having Pearly Gates as the benchmark, we designed a method to carve a niche for every instrument. There's a bit of novelty creating a cosmetically pleasing instrument: following the selection of woods, finishes, size, shapes, scale-lengths, hardware, electronics, wire gauge, and magnet strength, the construction proofs tell the tale. Listen . . . if it looks great, turn it up loud and that's that!

The master builders—John Bolin, Paul Reed Smith, Tom Anderson, Chandler, Tom Murphy, Mike Eldred, Matthew Kline, the guys at Fender, Seymour Duncan, the guys at Gibson, fabricators all over the world—can be quite fussy over these mechanical contraptions. Designs for ZZ Top's Worldwide Texas Tour guitar, the Texas-shaped one, were devised under the direction of Chuck Burge, operating the Gibson Custom Shop in Kalamazoo. Once the blueprints were completed, the guitar entered the fast lane. Important, as it was the first non-production instrument made at Gibson in 25 years. It's a Texas-size plank, a real beast!

STRINGS

Next to the guitar itself, strings are the next most important variable. I've experimented over the years with numerous string gauges. B. B. King opened my eyes to lighter gauges. Heavy strings are fine, yet not a necessity with sophisticated contemporary guitars and amps. Light-gauge strings are most effective. You just don't have to fight 'em as much. Ask Dunlop, Ernie Ball, Squire, or GHS—.008, .010, .012, .020, .030, .040. They hold up well. Even in the now-popular and lower-than-standard Spanish electric tuning, light strings can still be managed with a little extra care—one doesn't have to worry too much about wobbliness . . . or, you know, flop and drag.

String breakage is the great nemesis of every guitarist I know. That's just part of the program. String breakage in mid-solo is gonna happen, but when it does, it's just like driving an Italian sports car—you will arrive, maybe at a different time, but you will arrive!

AMPS

The other biggie is amplifiers. ZZ Top got satisfied early with Marshall, a couple stacks of 100-watt Super Leads. We also experimented with a host of other amps remaining in our collection. Some exotic tube-amp builders are wiring by hand, everything from 5 to 500 watts of usable power. Balls, Swanson, DST, Trinity, Texiana, 65, Chopper 18, Mojo, Ruby, Tone Tubby. ZZ's recent tours and television appearances have featured Ampeg's Crate V-50 combo . . . right on! Class A, 2x12, and 50 watts. Smokin' all!

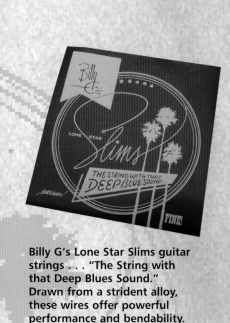

Billy G's Lone Star Slims guitar strings . . . "The String with that Deep Blues Sound." Drawn from a strident alloy, these wires offer powerful performance and bendability.

Popeye's Brand Electric Guitar Strings . . . this set is used mainly for Fender's 25 1/2-inch scale. And with these strings, the feel is heavy . . . oversized gauge. I like fried chicken, and with these strings, "The Grease is in The Grooves."

So, in other words, grab that slab, plug that sucker in, and grind me a pound. Make yo'se'f happy.

DAT'S WHAT BILLY F GIBBONS SAY.

BFG ready to rock the Crates; Summer '04.

JOHN BOLIN

Bolin Guitars' master builder has enjoyed a close association with Billy G. & Co., fabricating over 100 custom guitars and basses spanning more than two decades. John B. and Mr. G met in Boise, Idaho, just before a ZZ Top stage call for an appearance way back when. This is where Mr. Bolin picks up the story:

I introduced myself and said, "I make custom guitars."

Billy quickly shouted, "Get your best and I'll meet you in the green room in like 10 minutes."

I arrived a few minutes later and unzipped a couple of cases. Two minutes turned into 20, as he laid into both guitar and bass. Everyone's groovin' and so's Billy. I offered my card and 24 hours later we struck our first deal.

For the most part, we started the early projects with paper and pencil, making a few sketches, taking a few notes, and that's it. What's interesting is that everything--and I mean everything--is based around the guitar that's considered the Queen Guitar Almighty: Pearly Gates.

I'm as obsessed as Billy with tone and playability, and we've created some mighty mean gunslingin' geetars. As an example, Billy added Fender Esquires to the line-up. Yes, the elemental electric! Somewhat curious, I accepted his challenge to create a modified refit scale with some very specific dimensions. They worked out really well. We did an extensive makeover of these unusual creations, coloring them up with every shade under the sun, powering them with some heavy horsepower, and letting the doggone things bust loose.

Billy's mind's eye is really keen. A great sense of design and style that constantly stretches the boundaries for me as a guitar builder. I know he's always been ahead of time, in a sense. I don't know if he's on Cloud 9, Cloud "Something," or another planet. One thing I do know, he draws from a sense of history of what feels good in design, and on the sounds guitars make, as well. He takes it and looks forward. I think Billy actually reads the future a little bit, like he's looking into a crystal ball and seeing ahead. He may come up with an idea that's fully developed and by the time we complete the guitar, it's a thing that's like, "Wow. Where did this come from? Is it from the future . . . from the past?"

One of Billy's strengths in his approach to design is that all his guitars are timeless. His eye for detail is astounding. I've never seen anything quite like it. Invariably there's that spark of creativity followed by powerful ideas. A little bit of now, lots of vintage, and loads of what's going to happen! Billy had me make a pair of polished-stainless Tele-style guitars for his friends, Keith Richards and Ron Wood. Another ferocious design storm that went from scratchpad to a rock 'n' roll statement.

Billy has always stood above the rest in terms of his imagination and artistic delivery. In my opinion, he is one of the best of the legendary guitar players on the scene because of his ability to capture an audience in terms of tone, tenacity, and visuals. You'll always see something unusual at a ZZ Top show. He takes it to another level--he gives it a lot of color, leaving no stone unturned. He's very meticulous and it shows.

On these guitars--I mean all of our designs, all the color, all the jewelry--it's him. We've worked with different outlines and different materials. We've fabricated brass, bronze, aluminum. We've done carved tops, gold tops, flame tops, slab tops, warped tops, laid fur on the damn things. We've even built some see-through guitars outlined with neon for their videos. That was one of the craziest things we did, to say the least.

Last, Billy's been a partner and a real buddy who's been supportive of my family, and I look forward to sharing these instruments and new ideas that have blossomed from our friendship.

John Bolin with Bolin Guitars' Silver Sparkle Special. This guitar holds a 200 MPH land-speed record at the Bonneville Salt Flats. Speed-demon Mr. Roy Fjasted offered to load this one inside their '32 coupe and haul it down the line at the Flats! They busted the timing clock and made the club. And why not?!?! Buick portholes, metalflake paint . . . the consummate hot-rod guitar.

The *coup de grace*, this is the one! **Pearly Gates** in vintage presence. Nothing tampered with, nothing touched, all original. The cornerstone for **Billy F Gibbons** and the boys.

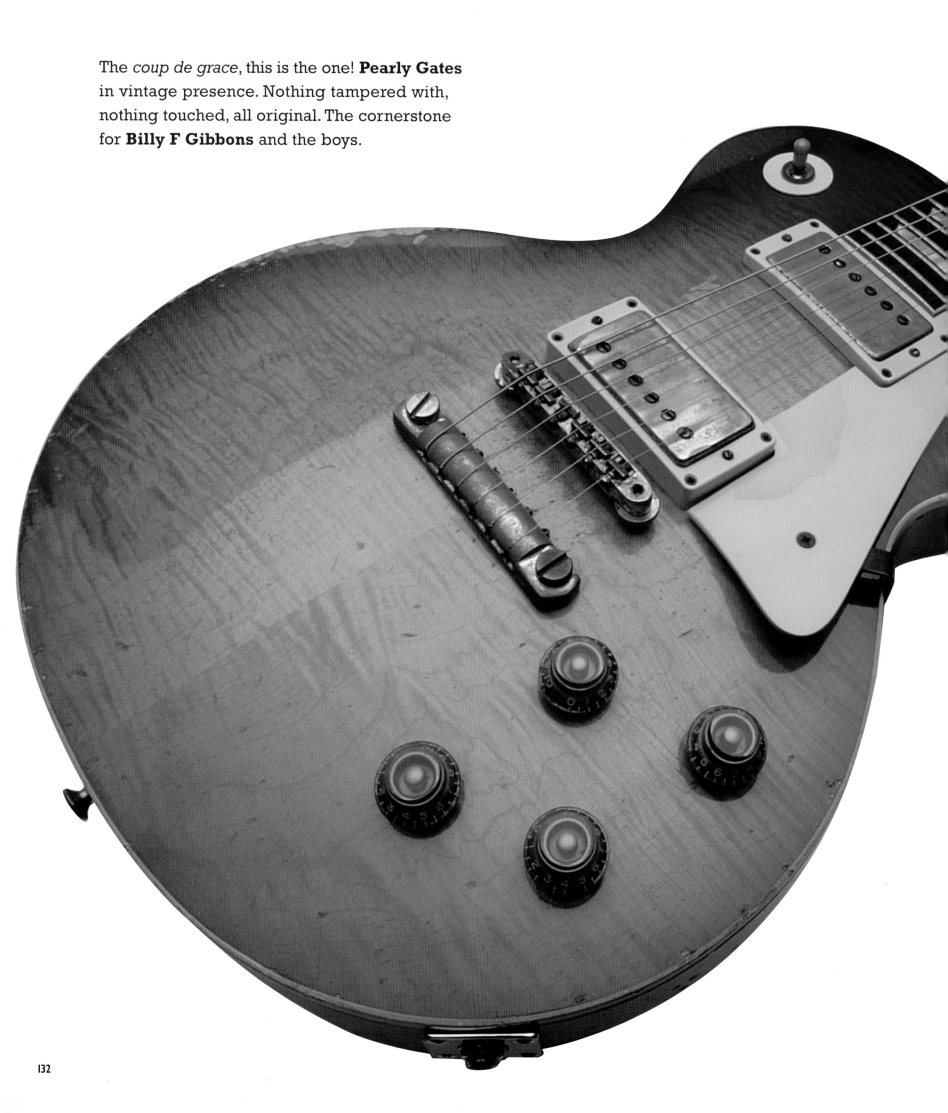

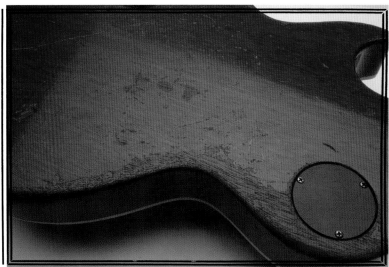

In their Nudie-fied glory, the boys be whippin' some wire!

Warmin' up in San Antone . . . dig Pearly and them custom amplifiers.

Same time, same grind . . . back to Pearly, let it rip!

The **1955 La Grange Fender Strat** . . . hardtail, no whammy. Straight stuff here! This particular thrasher, combined with **Pearly Gates**, harmonics included, put the crowning touch on **"La Grange."** Worn and weather-beaten, this skunk-striped, maple-necked special is another one that grooves on and on! Good combo.

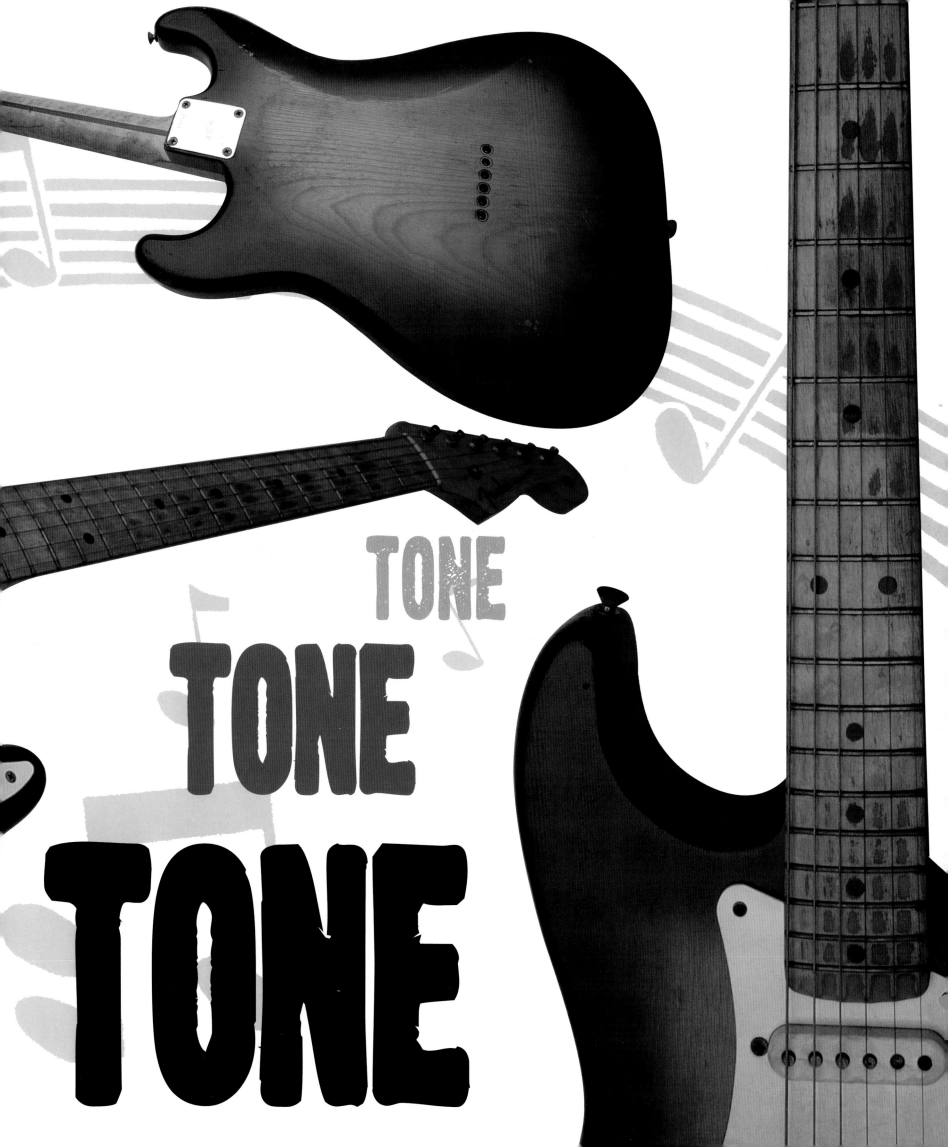

A pre-SG, **'61 Les Paul Standard** known as **Lil Red**. This is the "groove-approved"
VanTels' axe that inspired me to grab a *guitar* in the first place! **PAFs** (Patents
Applied For), correct controls, and some period-perfect hot-rod pinstriping . . .
Lil Red still thrives and plays like melting butter. Precious sound from this one.

An original **'58 Gibson Flying V**, the first guitar in the set outfitted with the yet-to-be-discovered twin humbucking pickups. Seeing **Clapton** pictured on the sleeve of **John Mayall's Bluesbreakers LP** holding a Gibson 'Burst with a **JTM 45** amp beside him was the signal to move in the humbucking direction. Makes sense . . . bigger pickup, bigger sound. African Limba Korina solid-body V, correct hardware, **PAFs**, and a sound that Albert King might be proud to play on . . . take note of the pink-colored hue on the pickguard, an anomaly found on the original series Flying Vs. The kneepad is intact and all elements are original. As seen on the cover of *Fandango*, this hunk can perform.

Early-'50s **Les Paul Goldtop** . . . this wretched wreck is featured prominently throughout the *Rhythmeen* sessions. As one may note, the replacement hardware was a result of some imminent thrashing. Need we say more?!

A '58 Les Paul 'Burst. Another rare but fine-sounding standard, heard on **"Just Got Paid."** It stays outfitted with extra-heavy strings and the action stays set high for bottleneck playing. This is a fierce performer slippin' around with a slither of a slide.

A vintage **'52 Fender Broadcaster**. This blackguard specialty remains all-original and is a nasty player. A deep V neck nearly plays itself from the low end to the top. This one got down on **"Jesus Just Left Chicago"** from *Tres Hombres*, way back in '73.

The **Alamo Fiesta**, made in San Antonio, 1960. This is the instrument heard on the track, **"Belt Buckle"** from the **XXX** album. Features a slimline, three-quarter-sized neck, with one half-coil pickup. Killer sound, killer player.

A rather beat-up and barbecued **National dobro** from the mid-'30s with a rare resonator cover plate. Originally issued as a painted guitar, years of heavy playing distressed the finish, creating an extraordinary patina. This particular instrument features a pearloid headstock, original "3-on-side" machine-heads, and a short-scale neck, joining at the 14th thread rather than the 12th, allowing easy access to the upper register. This instrument has a gut-bucket, throaty bottom end. Cuts like a knife.

A late-'30s **National Tricone**, and a rare example of a non-etched body. This one, refit with a custom-made neck, has been adorned with a superb inlay, images of **Bones and Lizards**. Precut pieces, shaken up by a local fortuneteller, like the reading of tea leaves, create a magnetically graphic inlay vision, a Mayan/lizard-like theme, cradling the yin and yang symbol. The words **"ZZ TOP"** adorn the center section. Again, another fine, resonator-electric hybrid. Typical of these innovative steel guitars circa the 1930s.

Found **in El Paso**, this is the lowdown-sounding **Pawn Shop Special** . . . with its original old Coke bottle-head and single silver lipstick pickup, this single-cutaway six can be heard on the ZZ Top cover of Elmore James' "Dust My Broom" from our first release for Warner Bros., *Degüello*, cut in 1979.

This interesting guitar is important for the presence of the **Rio Grande Valley**'s **Sun Valley Motor Hotel** room key, a laid-in reminder from the start, guitar style. This fine **Gibson** 'lectric was brought on board during the early touring days and the **Mexican border** gigs. Stand back and look out . . . this guitar shouted it out!

A nice maple-neck three-tone **Stratocaster** from **'56**, complete with fully sprung whammy bar. One of the classic examples of the **Fender** Strat. This particular one's behind the bluesy sound tracked on **"Apologies to Pearly"** from **ZZ's** *Rio Grande Mud*. Original electronics, Bakelite parts, and the deep "V" neck shape make this instrument way desirable. This one was injected to the set to add to the range of sounds additional to **Pearly Gates**.

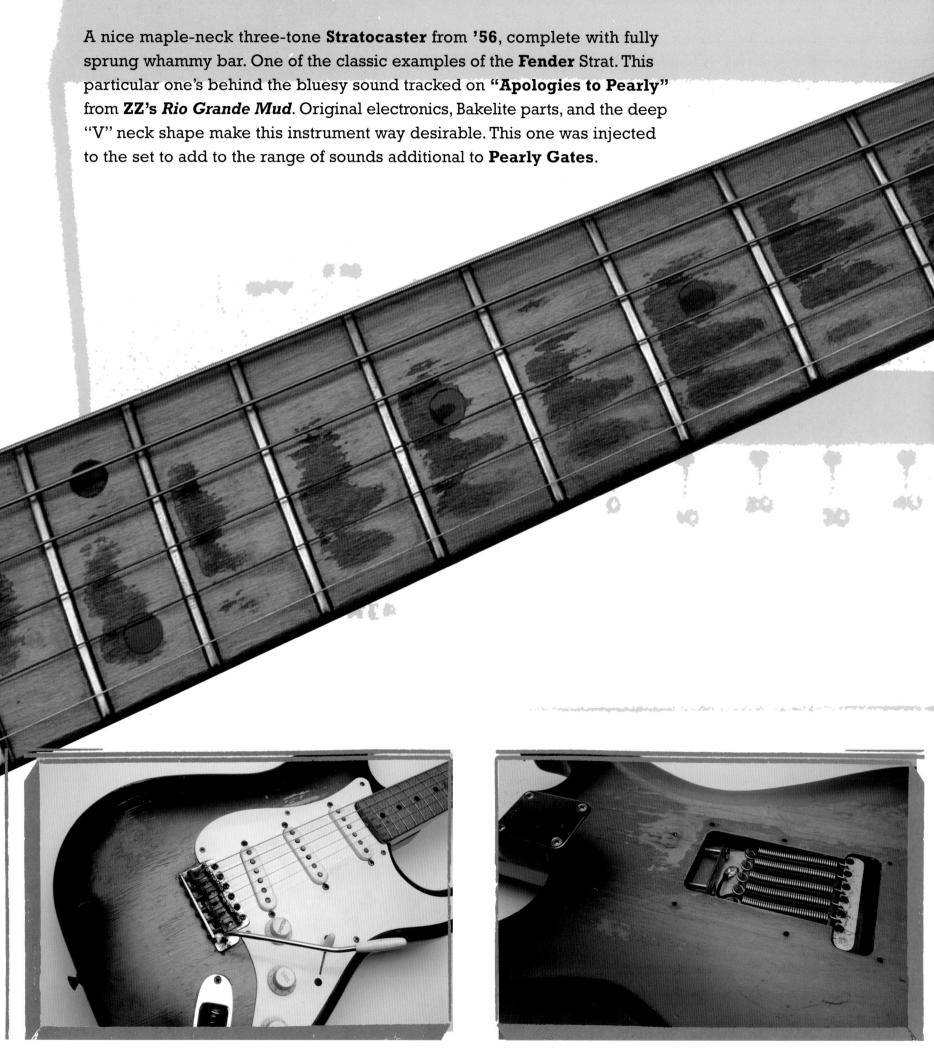

A **1955 Gretsch Roundup**. This stocker was used recording **"TV Dinners"** from the *Eliminator* LP.

The **1959 Gretsch** solid-body electric, originally named the **Jupiter Thunderbird**, now in the Gretsch line as the **Billy-Bo** was dreamed up by none other than **Bo Diddley** . . . **Frank Lloyd Wright** meets **Mississippi Mud**. This being one of three known to have been made in '59 for Bo & Co. All important injections into pop culture—true contemporary architecture and design. A treasured gift from **Bo Diddley** and a welcomed addition to the set. Quite an imaginative guitar.

Billy and the lovely Gilligan atop of Palm Springs Highway 111 with the infamous Billy-Bo Gretsch given to BFG by Bo Diddley.

The **Gretsch** "back-engineered" **Billy-Bo**, mirror-image design now offered in its non-reverse form and instigated by none other than **Bo Diddley**! It features the original configuration of two **Filtertron** pickups, **Space-Control** bridge, a "G" tailpiece, string-thru body construction, a speed demon four-knob configuration, and a three-position toggle switch. One satirical addition on this **"Reverso"** is the backward-reading headstock logo! This one's seen some tough and tight touring down the roads. It's both comfortable and playable . . . meat on metal on wood.

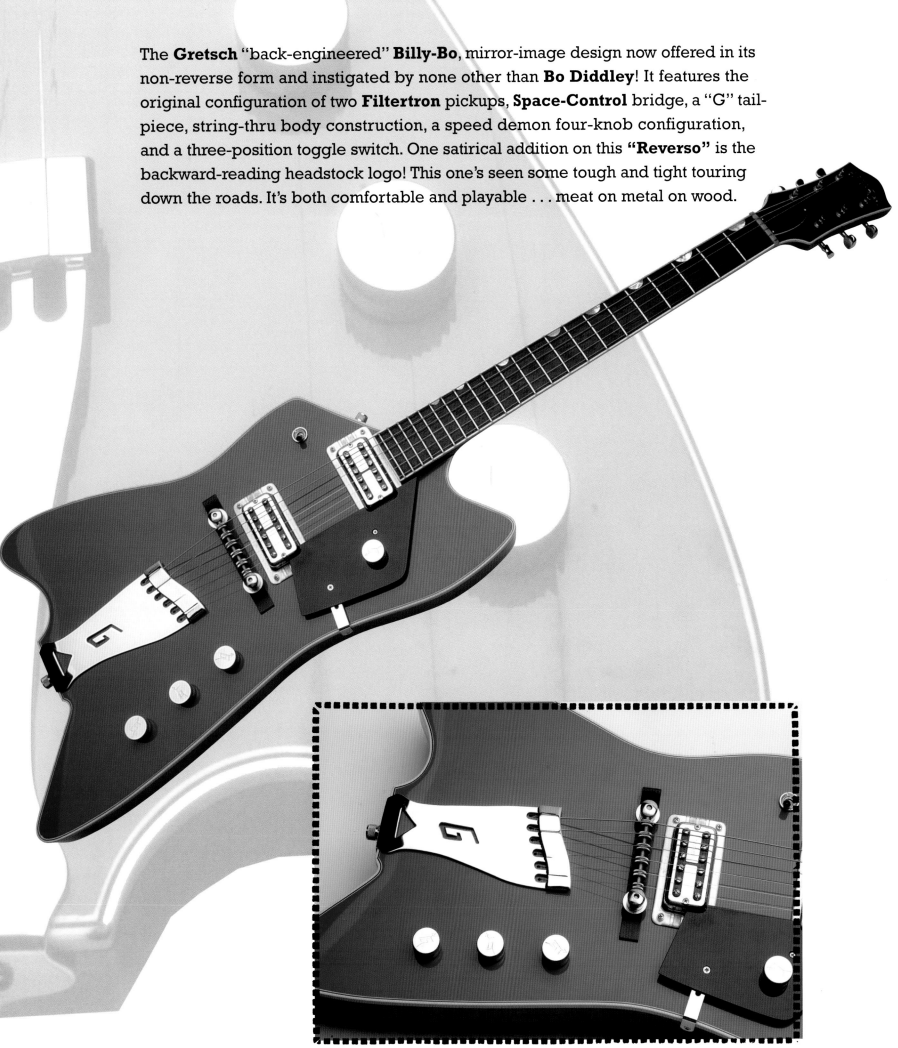

the BOLD

An **early-'60s Magnatone Zephyr**. Another excursion into special effects, this particular version placed a pair of **Bixonic Expandora** stomp boxes onboard to add a special fuzz within the output. Two punchy single-coil pickups plus a solid slab-body with a whammy bar in the middle of it all, make this instrument quite fascinating. Played live onstage throughout **ZZ Top's** *Recycler* tour.

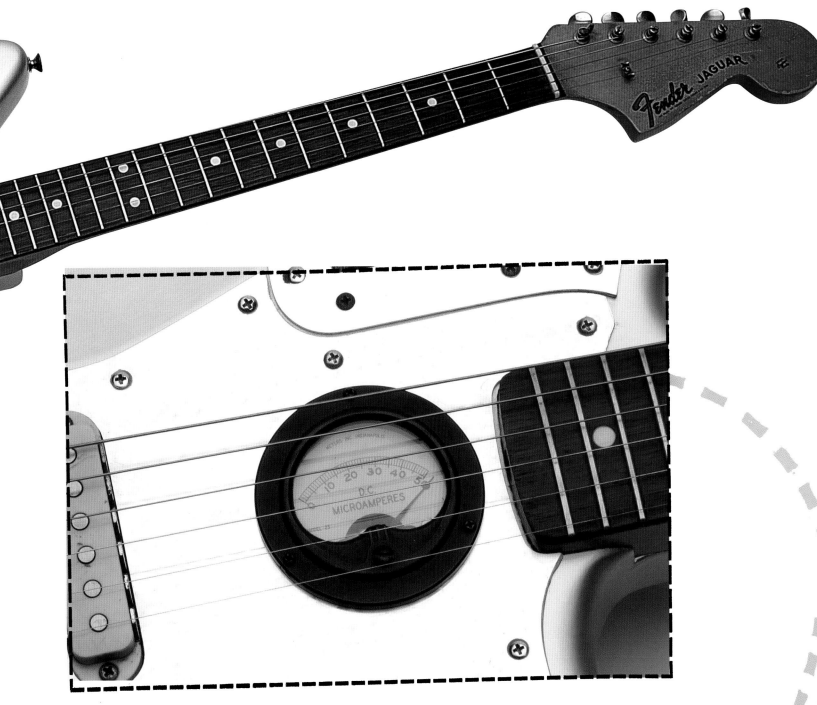

This is the **'65 California Jaguar** that was customized and modified in Fullerton around 1969. "Rick's" . . . the surf-shop-sticker'd guitar. One bridge pickup, engine-turned metal pickguard shielding onboard, signal-boosting circuitry, and there's a light-up dial under strings, which, though visibly pleasing, is totally useless. Who's gonna look at a gauge needle in the heat of a rippin' moment of madness?! A weird piece in guitar design history. This instrument, acquired in '73, is heard on three tracks recorded for the *Tejas* album. Choice axe.

and the Beautiful

A **Moving Sidewalks**-era piece and yet another version what **Bo Diddley** started years before, the fur-covered axe. This one, a conglomerate of extra-wide **Jazzmaster** pickups, an **ABR-1** bridge, a **Tele**-style string-thru body, and imitation sheepskin fur . . . well . . . it's a cool one. Fluorescent green sunburst finish and construction details were handily managed by **Moving Sidewalks** bassist **Mr. D. F. Summers**. This one's emblazoned in mind and plays great.

Poster announcing an early Sidewalks engagement.

THE
**MOVING
SIDEWALKS**
SCEPTER-WAND RECORDING ARTISTS
Houston **TEEN-AGE
FAIR 1967**

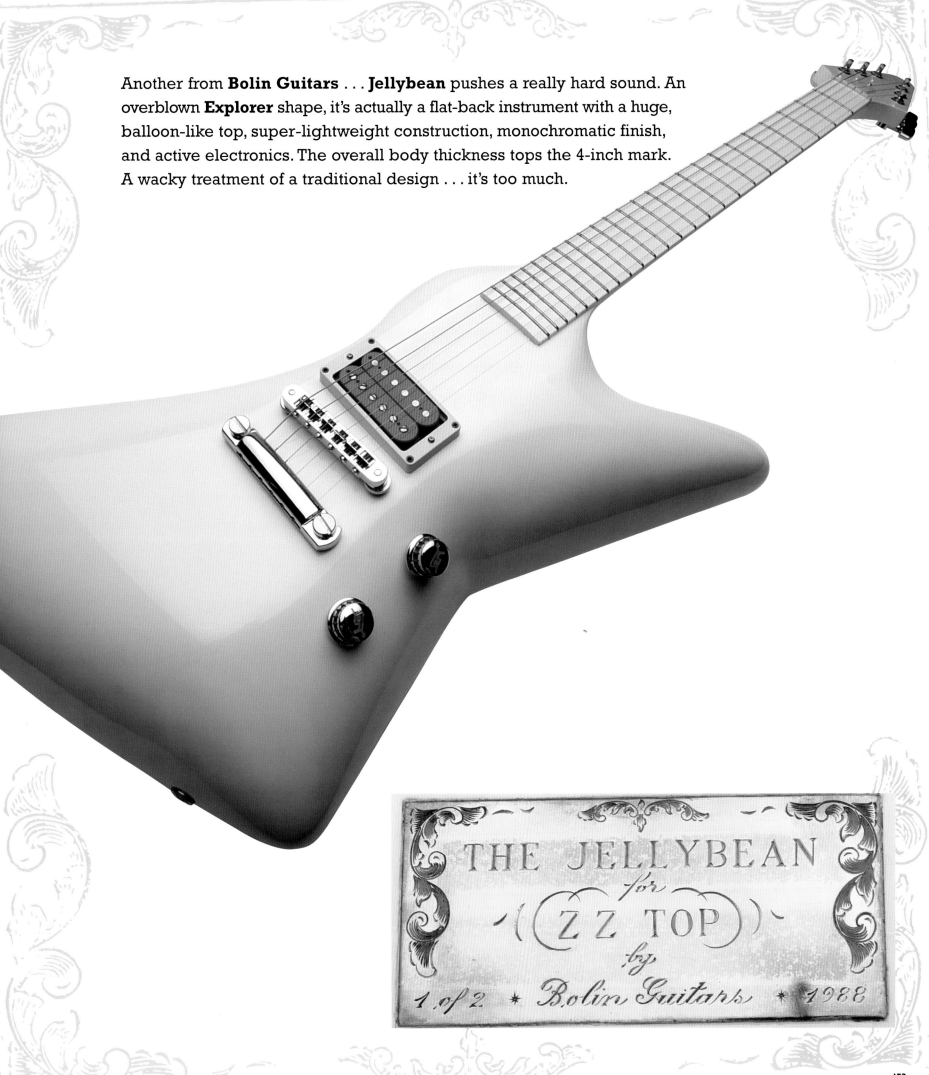

Another from **Bolin Guitars** . . . **Jellybean** pushes a really hard sound. An overblown **Explorer** shape, it's actually a flat-back instrument with a huge, balloon-like top, super-lightweight construction, monochromatic finish, and active electronics. The overall body thickness tops the 4-inch mark. A wacky treatment of a traditional design . . . it's too much.

THE JELLYBEAN
for
ZZ TOP
by
1 of 2 ∗ Bolin Guitars ∗ 1988

This custom half-scale solid body is a tight-sounding box, designated for that six-string thing . . . **"I'm Bad, I'm Nationwide."** Really tight, full tone.

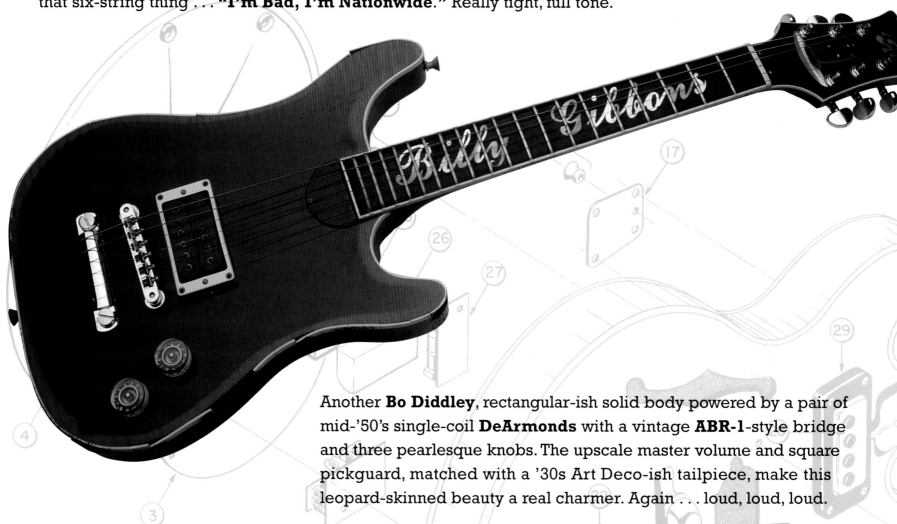

Another **Bo Diddley**, rectangular-ish solid body powered by a pair of mid-'50's single-coil **DeArmonds** with a vintage **ABR-1**-style bridge and three pearlesque knobs. The upscale master volume and square pickguard, matched with a '30s Art Deco-ish tailpiece, make this leopard-skinned beauty a real charmer. Again . . . loud, loud, loud.

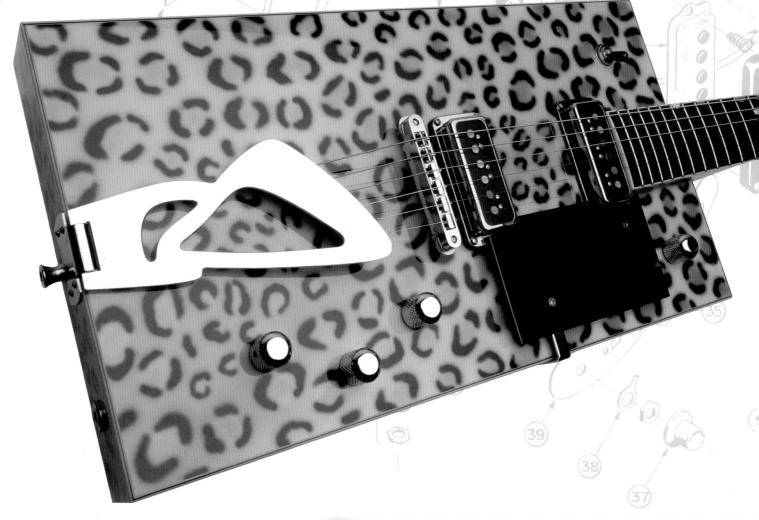

An interesting item from the **Gibson Custom Shop**, this is a stop-tailpiece **Les Paul Goldtop** with one **P-90 pickup** in the bridge position. It's got an original, '58 Thunderbird hood badge, inspired by the recording of **"Thunderbird"** on the *Fandango* release. African brew is immortalized on this guitar with **"Drink Mamba Beer"** inlaid on the fingerboard. Kinda sudsy.

A creation from street artist **Eric Yunker** of San Francisco, a talented scavenger who used "found" parts to make his unusual creations. This six-string jewel was highlighted on the cover of *Guitar Player Magazine* for the feature **"The Guitar as Art."** Rather clunky and heavy, it's still playable and invites an excursion of the wire into places unknown. A strange instrument from an engineering genius . . . sliding pickups, retro tuners, and finger-controlled volume and wah-wah knobs. Take note of the Westinghouse leveling springs and Dodge Ram hood ornament as the positioning stretch at the rear of the instrument. Quite exotic.

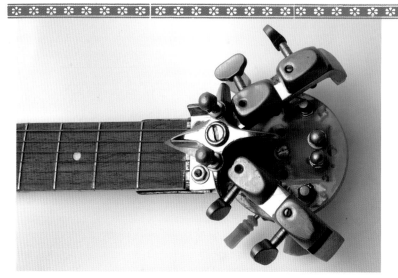

A fine example of **Fender's "Esquire**-ing" elegance, rolled out of the **Fender Custom Shop** around the *Mescalero* sessions in 2002. This particular one, the latest in a series of a half-dozen started in 1990 and nicknamed **Alley-Gator**, was used on the track of the same name. Fully loaded, extra-fancy binding, and the top and sides have a blue-pearled thunderbolt inlay across the body and down the neck. Ebony 'board, lightweight ash body. Smooth. **TONE**.

CUSTOM MADE BY
GIBSON
FOR
BILLY GIBBONS
1979 C.T.Burge
Designer / Luthier

BFG and the six-string homage to Tejas, as seen in a '70s tour program.

Featured here is an important offering from the rare days of **Gibson**'s willingness to create a custom-made first class instrument. This one being the now-famed **Lone Star Slim Special**, the Texas-shaped electric from 1979. This was the first custom-made instrument to emerge from the Gibson factory in **Kalamazoo** in some 20-odd years. Details of this instrument, recorded in the Gibson archive, reveal some of the guitar's unusual design aspects and applications. Under the direction of **Chuck Burge**, appointed to head the new Special Projects Department, this oversized super became a reality. It was outfitted with another Gibson rarity: an active circuit that added onboard signal-boosting to the twin humbucking line on command. It's a fancy item for sure . . . bound-mahogany body, neck, and headstock, Brazilian rosewood fingerboard, gold hardware, all the extra trimmings to make this one a Wild West electric. Still big as Texas. . . and smokin'.

This is the **ZZ Top Crazy Cowboy**, another **Bolin**, made in '89. A giant **Switchmaster** neck-thru body coupled to a **Firebird** reversed headstock, rear-mounted single knob, and pickup with **Trini Lopez's** diamond body cavities from the '60s. It's a big player.

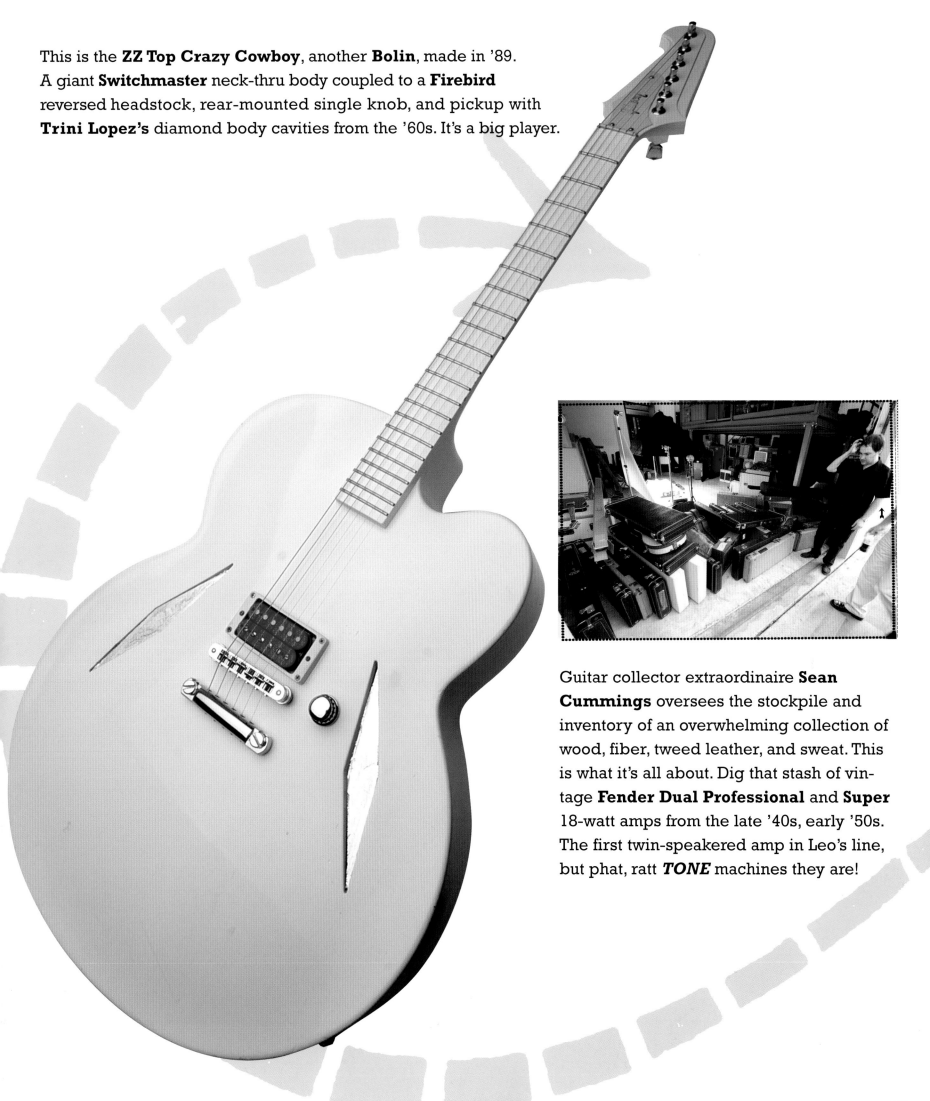

Guitar collector extraordinaire **Sean Cummings** oversees the stockpile and inventory of an overwhelming collection of wood, fiber, tweed leather, and sweat. This is what it's all about. Dig that stash of vintage **Fender Dual Professional** and **Super** 18-watt amps from the late '40s, early '50s. The first twin-speakered amp in Leo's line, but phat, ratt *TONE* machines they are!

This is the **Bolin Guitars** expression of "Tuff meets Tiki" . . . the elegance of a single pickup powering the bamboo body and neck speaks of rustic times. The simplicity of a "war club" design ethic makes it purely primitive. This guitar brought a supercharged aim to the recording direction of the **Rhythmeen** sessions. Exotic and hypnotic.

DESCRIPTION

MRB Switch (Momentary)
Decorative Nut
Switch (Tremolo/Reverb)
Metal Housing
. . . Plate & Tread A
Pedal Cable
Pedal As
Phono
De

Transformer (Power)
Control Panel (Only)
Transformer (Reverb)
Transistor (Power)
Transformer (Driver)
Transistor (Power)
Capacitor (Filter)
Capacitor (Filter)

This unusual instrument was created in Houston by **Airline Guitars**, from **Axhandle Guitar Works**. This crazy contraption, a two-piece neck, divided by a **Mini-14** flash muzzle, leaves the headstock section separate and independently tuned from the main neck. Both neck sections are active, with a **Piezo** pickup under the headstock and wired to the bridge pickup, making both sections playable at the same time. The top end side of the neck is tuned open, while the main section of the instrument is tuned and played traditionally . . . an unorthodox combination, perhaps, but great for bottlenecking. Radical. Takes two hands and a lot of hammerin'.

This is a famous one from **Steve Metz**'s **"Scientifico Musico Technographique."** This surrealist guitar is another great-sounding axe. The unusual outline exhibits a sort of Egyptian quality, coupled with a "new-traditionalist" hot-rod feel with the machine-turned pickguard, and a drilled-out Phoenician-looking headstock. A kind of **Fellini**-esque application, going back to guitar design of the **early '50s**. Stand back and stare!

This bright-green, custom-made beauty was crafted especially for **Mr. Dusty Hill**, bassist, and his minimalist guitar style. Particularly important, this **Crop Duster Special** is the instrument heard on the rhythm track in the song **"Breakaway,"** featuring the bearded Mr. Hill playing in fine form. The high-powered **EMG** pick-up allowed The Dust to be particularly expressive outside of his famous four-string bass guitar arena, bringing his special-order six-string to the rodeo. A very special guitar. A gift from the Dusty Hill collection.

A twisted, demented shape gives rise to this most unusual creation, called **La Warpa**. One pickup, one knob, and a curved, solid body carved out of a 6-inch block of mahogany. It's a real **Dali**-esque twist. Almost awkward to perform with, but a splendid acid-like view is had by all.

Here's another **Bo Diddley**-inspired alien. This beautiful **Gretsch** has authentic **Von Dutch** pinstriping on the face! This is the kind of guitar that offers the hillbilly, rockabilly, Rock 'n' Roll, Blues guy the chance to fire up the rig and put the pedal to the metal. Pure hot rod and plays like purple velvet! Check out one of these grit and grindin' Gretsch groove boxes . . . like a fine plate of **El Compadre** enchiladas.

A custom offering from the artistic talents of **Bernard Moix**, **Switzerland**'s leading exponent of cars, guitars, motorcycles, and pretty girls. This one was fabricated in the fine tradition of my **1950 Ford** kustom, **Kopperhed**. This classically styled instrument features a rolled and pleated pickguard, a machined engine-styled valve-cover bridge, Ford key ignition switch, single knob, and a single pickup arrangement. The guitar, nicknamed **KruiZZerhed**, is a righteous machine . . . an original set of **Kluson** tuning keys, a round-button '50s string retainer, an engine-turned control plate, and the specially numbered pearl inlay position markers complement the 1950 baby Ford hubcap. Surrounded with hot-rod details, this beach beauty evokes the pleasures of pop, hop, and bop.

Los Angeles pop . . . **Snake and Bones Esquire**. This particular guitar adds another feature to the previous example of simplicity. A two-knobbed, single-stacked-humbucking-pickup, solid-body electric, it features exotic silverwork from the famed L.A. silversmith **Gabor**, a radical Hungarian guy who brought a style of silversmithing to high fashion and pop. This particular piece remains among my most-valued, signifying personal relationships with **Gabor**, **Ryk Maverick's Starlingear**, **Bill Wall**, **Travis Walker**, **Reed Rowland**, **Richard Stark**, **Dennis Pollicino**, **Jerry Van Amberg**, and **Alan Glynn**'s **Harleywood** motorcycle showroom and shop, when the hang was down on **La Brea Avenue** . . .

This important piece is also one of the highlights from the collection because it appeared as the silver jewelry scene was unfolding in the early '90s. Truly a piece of genuine **West Coast** originality and aesthetic. Note closely **"Laguna Beach Love Gun"** engraved in the Snake and Bones hunk of .995 pure silver . . . **Gabor's** enlightened touch. An important piece from a most eccentric shaper of silver. *Beer Drinkers and Hell Raisers*!

Here's a super-streamlined example of one of a pair made as gifts for ZZ's guitar-playin' pals, **Mr. Dwight Yoakam** and **Mr. Pete Anderson**. Where would we be without **Buck Owens**!? This is the hot-rod version, **Moon Eyes** decal included. Think "Buck Owens" and play it right!

The rhinestoned **Explorer**-like solid, one of two made for
the **ZZ Top** *Eliminator* tour. Featuring a solid face of
sparkling stones covering the ebony body. Again, this is
another creation with simplicity—one volume control,
Seymour Duncan's "buckpink" **Pearly**-wound pickup,
and a **Flying V**-styled headstock. Matching bass.
Bolin Guitars, 1983.

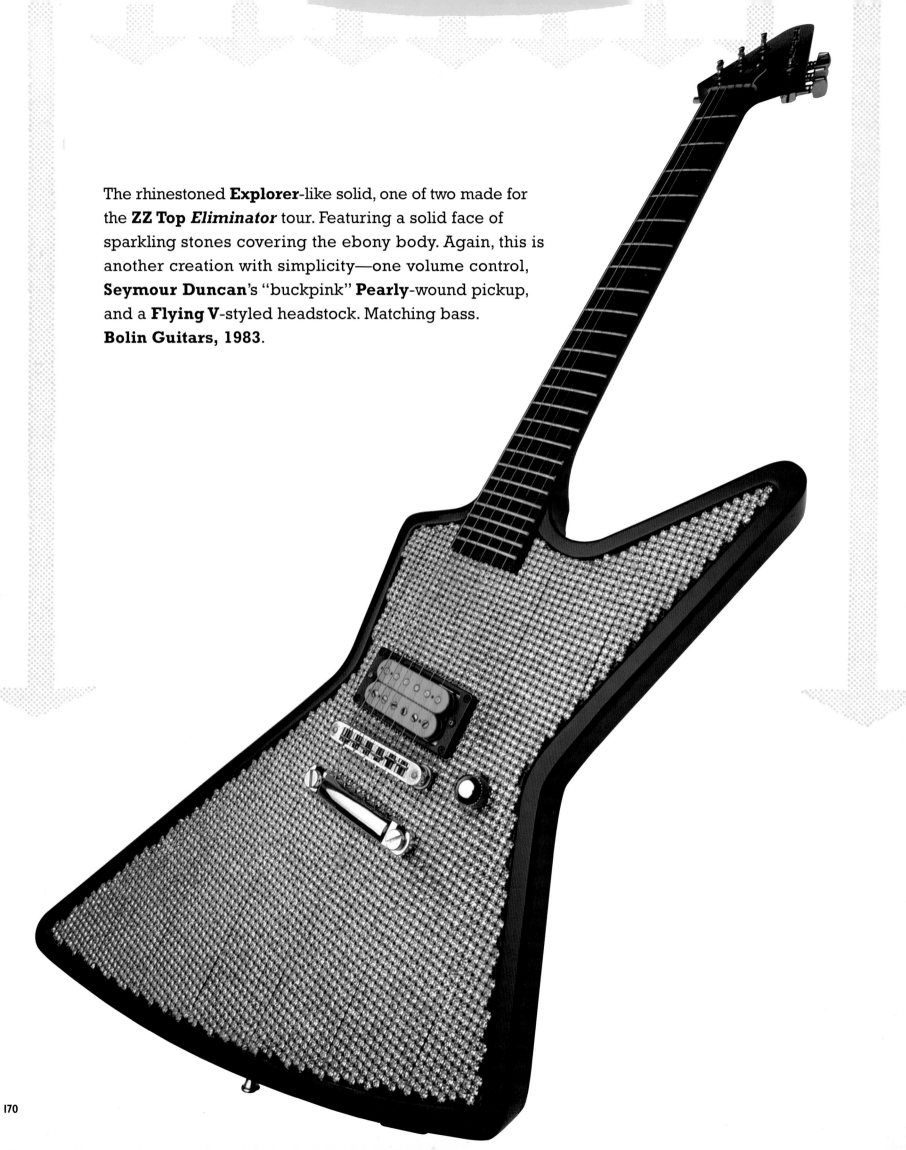

The Dizzy One. Again, an extreme example of the famous **Explorer** shape, this one adorned with a 3-D laminate covering the entire top, neck, and headstock. Once again, **Seymour Duncan** wound the wire with his notorious **Pearly Gates** model pickup. **Jim Rice**'s custom speed knob and a **Flying V**-styled headstock keep this one in fine form. The name badge says it all . . .

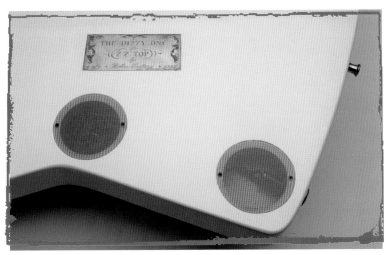

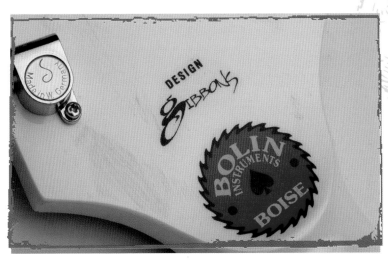

GrooveBox *in reverse* . . . a customized, carved-top, mahogany **Esquire**. Some not-often-seen checkerboard binding around the guitar highlights the inlay, **"xoBevoorG"**. This is the favorite, marked "#8".

Another version of the **Crazy Cowboy** guitar, this one's a heavyweight. No cost for the high gloss, the talents and shop work tapped from **Bolin Guitars** hand-hammered the solid 24-carat gold-leaf peace-symboled arched top. Added to its solid-goldness is a pushbutton, onboard wireless transmitter. A fine piece of guitar glitz.

21Balls, a brightly lit custom instrument, best described as an escapee from the film *Earth Girls Are Easy*. This instrument requires quite a bit of external power to flash the illuminated numerals inlaid within each one of the spherical circles. The convergence near the neck is worth the price of admission alone.

21Balls and a pair of Billy's travel-axe cuties to boot!

A custom from the **Hamer** factory, this one in the **Explorer** tradition with a geometrically stylized angle cut on the body and headstock. Taking shapes from diamond faceting, it's a no-frills electric. The one unusual addition are LEDs flat in the fret board, lit up as the strings are struck. This, too, is a bitchin' player.

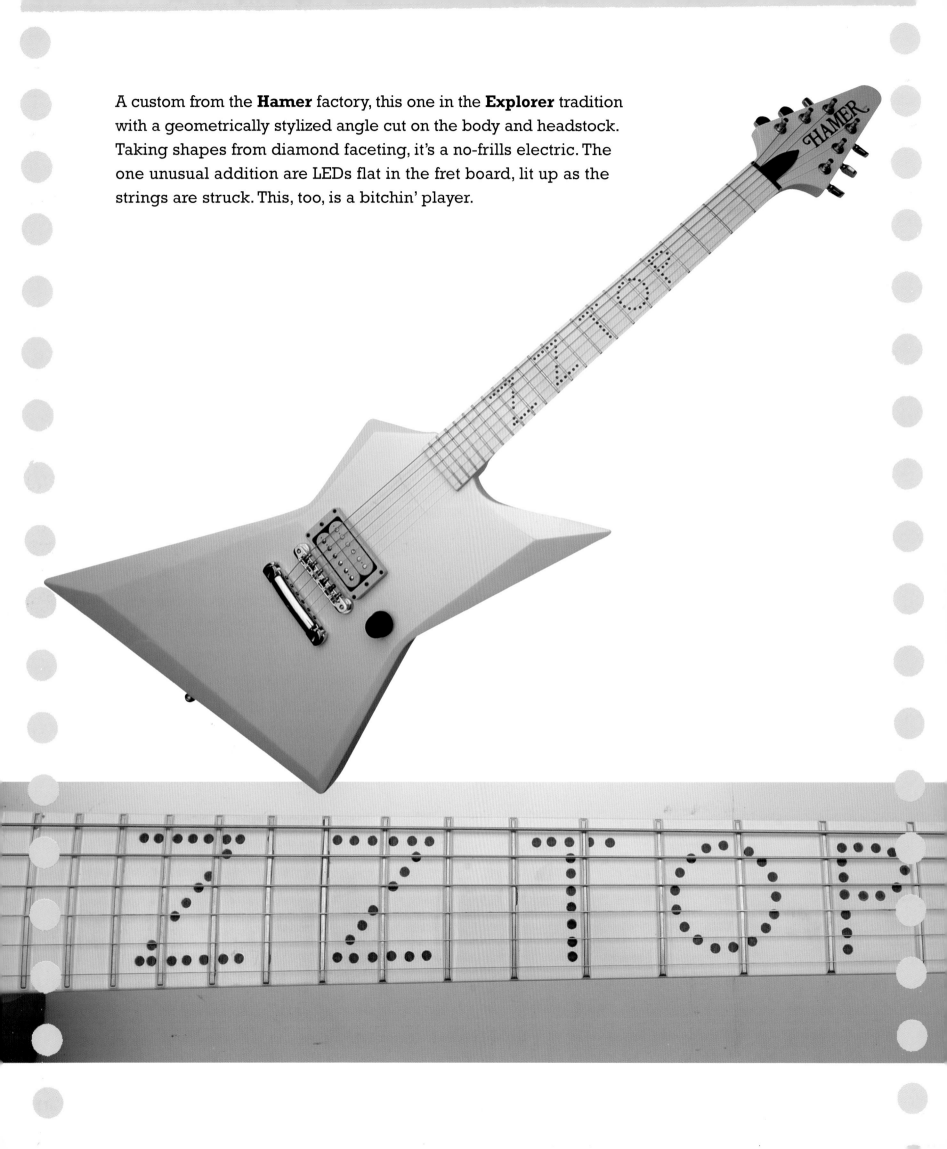

A dual-purpose double-neck featuring a long-scale and short-scale neck combination, tethered to the **BFG Studios** adjustable bridges and the thru-body tuning keys at the headstocks. Some bold pearl inlay, referencing the longstanding nickname **"Reverend Willy G."** This guit' piece is noteworthy . . . carved top body, blade volume slider, two well set-up necks . . . listen closely to **"Low Down In The Street."** This twin-neck plays twice!

The Reverend Willy G. . . . bein' bad and nationwide!

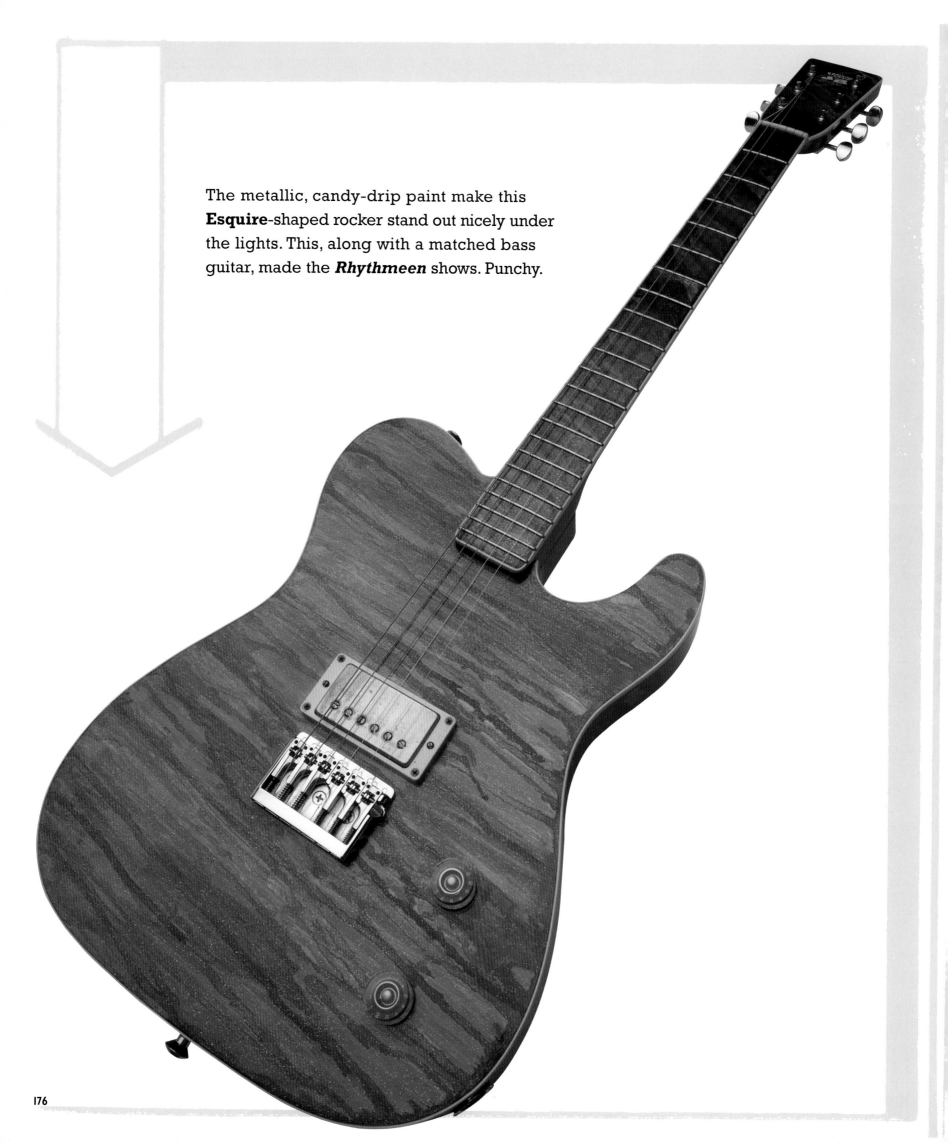

The metallic, candy-drip paint make this **Esquire**-shaped rocker stand out nicely under the lights. This, along with a matched bass guitar, made the *Rhythmeen* shows. Punchy.

The famous **Furry One**. In 1983, **Gibson Guitar Company** honored our request to create a customized fur guitar and matching bass for the video "Legs." The designers, **Matthew Kline** and **Mike McGuire**, selected an **Explorer** shape with gold-plated hardware and **Seymour Duncan**'s buckpink **Pearly Gates** winding, and covered the completed pieces with imitation sheepskin. Here 'tiz! The instrument itself is built from solid mahogany and has the trademark **ZZ Top**-painted rosewood fingerboard. The machine heads were manicured with beauty salon hair ties . . . gotta keep that fur in place. They spin and they actually play great.

Billy's Bo Diddley-inspired brainchild . . . the first Furry One.

One of the more interesting examples of a **late-'30s National steel**. This resonator instrument features some contemporary pearl inlay with a fine version of the traditional **"Tree of Life"** pattern up the neck and a mysterious, Mayan-like petroglyphic lizard holding the yin and yang symbol laid in two-toned shades of pearl. This particular "Nash" has been well played and well beaten up . . . a groove-a-licious grindstone, to say the least.

A matched **Strat** and **Precision** bass were dreamed up for the first ZZ Top video, **"Gimme All Your Lovin,'"** when headless guitars were making the scene. Stock Fenders were taken off the shelf to the workshop backroom where the headstocks were immediately hacked off! The pinstripes were part of ZZ Top's fixation on hot rods, so on went the lines. The white finish and tortoiseshell pickguards are pure '60s Fender. How do you tune this thing!? Not exactly playable, but who cares?! This is the movies . . .

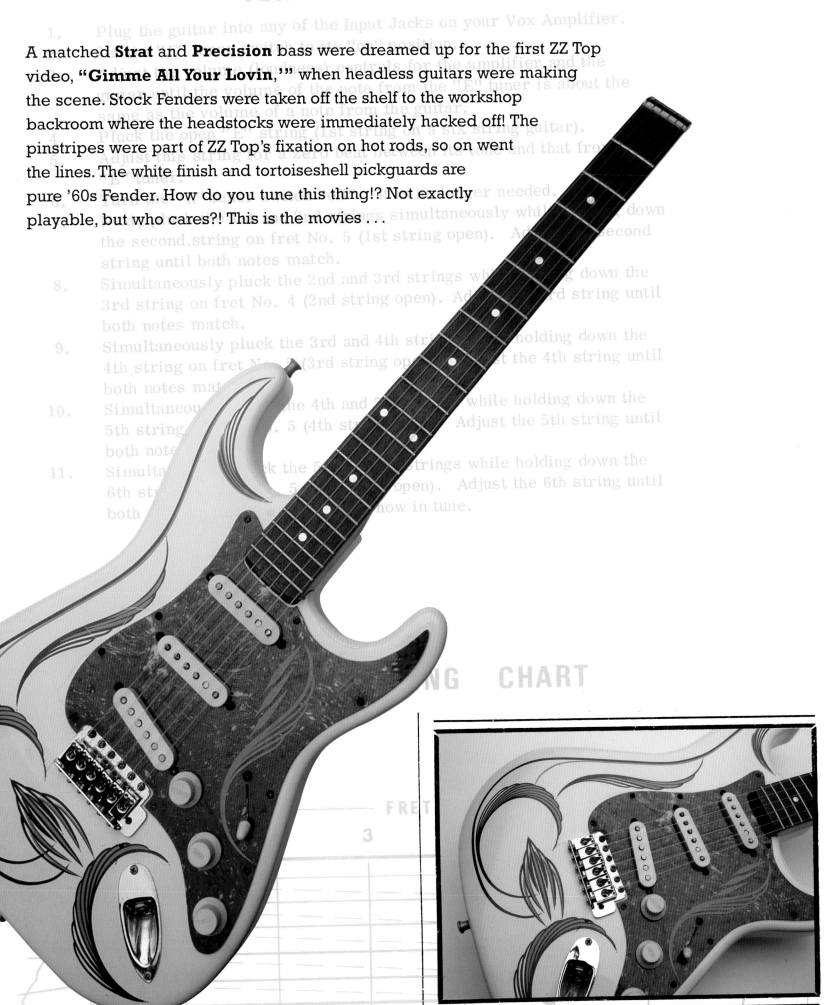

This is a **'55 Fender Strat** is covered in cowhide applied in the custom shop by the crew at **Bill Wall Leather** up in Malibu. Their work can't be beat! Check out their sterling silver hardware on this vintage one. We used the **Cowhide Special** on the track **"Black Fly"** from *Rhythmeen*.

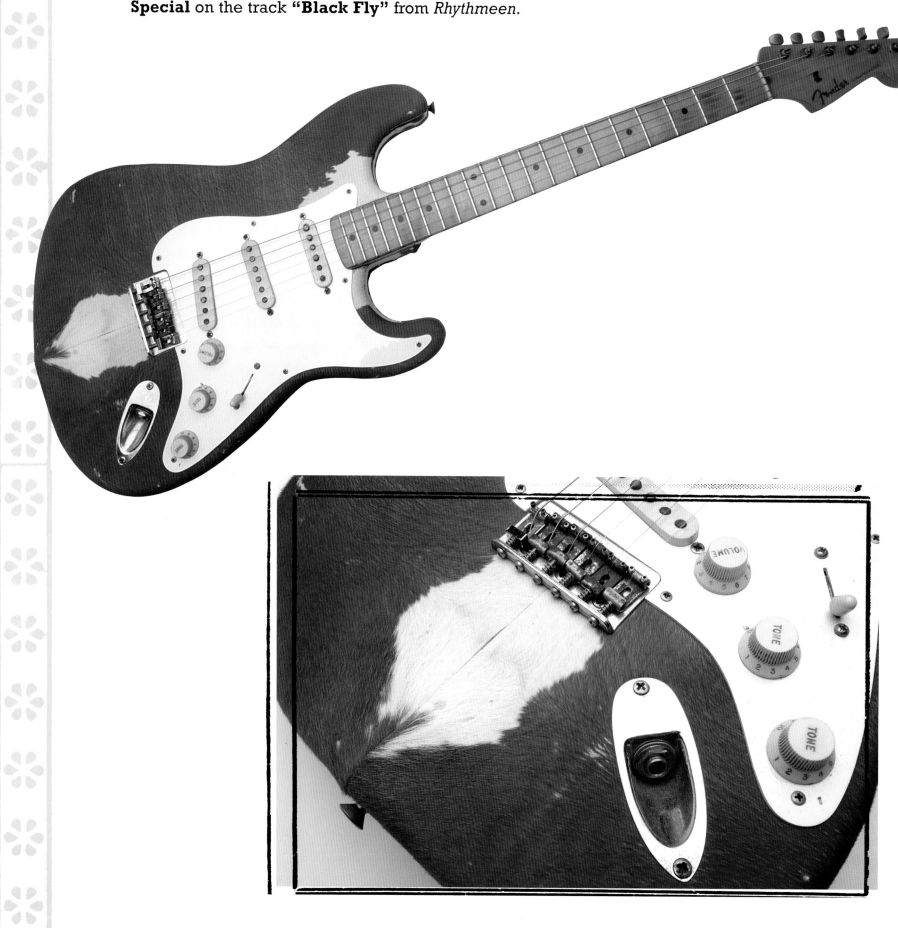

Our good friend and guitarmaker from **Paris** and **L.A.**, **Monsieur James Trussart**, handcrafted these **Esquire-meets-National** instruments. The metal body's weather-distressing and the chambering through the top made it retro resophonic traditional. A late-model ashtray anchors the strings to a short-scale neck. The inlay, crafted by **Dave Nichols' Pearl Works** points to an affection for African languages . . . roughly translated, **"Billy Bwa"** became Trussart's **"Billy Boy."** This instrument and a matching bass were televised on the **Billboard Music Awards** in **Vegas**. The machine-worked resonator grilles, à la '30s style, stretch across the top *and* through the sides of the metal body, resonating with killer sustain.

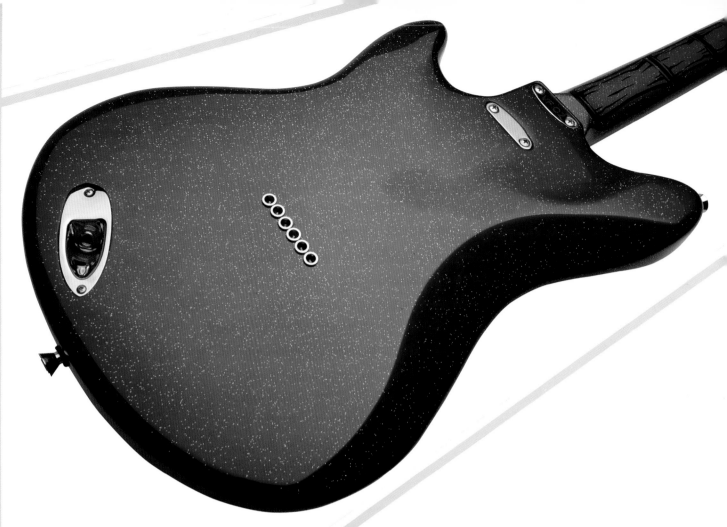

Here's the **Hawaiian**-inspired solid-body electric conceived by **Paul Chandler** and hot-rod artist **Von Franco**. This one, called the **Taboo Tiki**, has a flamed, stylized tiki design rear of the bridge. The convenient feel of this guitar comes from Chandler's innovative, rear-body neck scalloping, the double-pinned neck joint, and the rear-mounted **Strat**-styled input jack. The string-thru body fab makes for harder string tension and long sustain. The tiki continues on the backside with bamboo outlines running heel to headstock. Aloha!

Here's another delivered out the back door of the **Gibson Custom Shop**. A modified **'61 Les Paul**. This one, outfitted with one **PAF** pickup and two knobs, and retaining the rather infamous "hydraulic" vibrato bar, revisiting a **Keith Richards "SG-meets-Flying V"** special. Check out the completed project here. Additionally, the instrument is laid with "steel-pearl" barbed-wire inlay, matched at both ends of the fretboard with religiously inspired Celtic cross icons. Repositioning of the input, volume, and tone knobs placed the visual impact of the guitar on its own plane.

One of the series of eight instruments called **The Shiv**, a **BFG** suggestion and challenge to **Bolin Guitars'** "**House of JB**." This particular example was the mainstay of the *XXX* tour, and the rustically carved, primitive African styling works well with the blades lifted from a Mexicana gift shop. Play it like you slay it!

Built in 1986, an extremely rare one-off, a hand-made piece from **PRS**, another great guitar-building manufactory from the U.S.A. An **Explorer**-styled instrument finished in pearl white lacquer across the body and neck, one bridge pickup, one knob. Signed and dated by **Paul Reed** Smith. A smoking player of a guitar no matter where you go.

Another interesting **Esquire**-esque offering with flowing pearl inlay. Just stark, minimalist simplicity. And another loud shouter wired with **Duncan Pickup**'s expertise.

From the year 2000, here's a choice steel-mill unit from the quiet, tucked-away **Teuffel Guitar Shop** in Germany's **outback**. Dubbed the *Birdfish*, this headless, scary marvel stakes a completely customized array of three-positionable pickups . . . North, South, East, and West. Reverse-mounted tuning keys and interchangeable tone chambers make this one a most noteworthy addition. With tone to the bone, this one was definitely "a keeper." Matching bass guitar.

The Muddywood built by **Pyramid Guitars** in **Memphis**. This Blues-playin' classic was glued together from the roof timber of **Muddy Waters'** cabin in **Clarksdale**, **Mississippi**. Ya' gotta imagine the **Mississippi River** winding down the body, down the neck, flowing right on into the Gulf. The rust-colored river, outlined agro-green, is like the muddy waters of the Mississippi. Let's hit it!

¡Muchas gracias, mi compañeros!

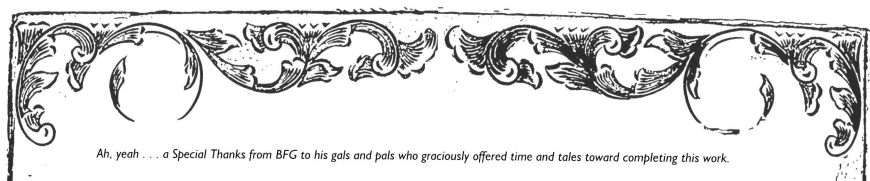

Ah, yeah . . . a Special Thanks from BFG to his gals and pals who graciously offered time and tales toward completing this work.

¡Muchas gracias, mi compañeros! I want to acknowledge, firstly, my mates, Frank, Dusty, and Bill, for their faithful friendship and for being there on this amazing journey.

"TV" Tom Vickers for guiding the way through the many experiences found within these pages. Mr. Dennis Pernu, who assisted in the preparations for this grand excursion, and who gladly sampled Rev. Willy's Renegade Guacamole in San Antonio.

Mr. David Perry, whose creative custom car vision can't be beat. Mr. John Bolin of Bolin Guitars, who stands as one of our favorite master guitar blaster builders. And the extra-special guitar specialists who offered action for acquisitions in the electric arena: George Gruhn, Alex Guitarzza, the *Vintage Guitar* gang, *Tone Quest Magazine*, *Guitar Player* and *Guitar World*, both the best in complete guitar liveliness. My standby tech-spec specialists, Elwood Francis, Billy Hale, and Johnny Douglas. Joe Hardy and G. L. G-Mane Moon, engineering experts who perfected the recordings with the Billy-Bo Gretsch. Mike Lewis, who made the Billy-Bo a reality. Bob Merlis, Mr. PR Deluxe. The El Paso Gringo Peligroso, Mr. Sean "Guitar" Cummings.

My loyal assistant, Denise. Bob Haynes and his Wrench Wranglers. Mr. "CarArt" Thom Taylor for the vintage speed ads. Big Jon Luhrs for the fine line guitar renderings. My sweetie, the lovely Ms. Gilligan Stillwater. Brandon "TipTop" Stanton, who scouted the locations far and wide. The superb silver jewelry sensation who keeps us nice and shiny, Mr. Ryk Maverick. My favorite H-town crowd: Little Miss AlleyCat, Lawrence Berry, J. P. "Outta Control" Shellnutt, and Rafael Cisneros down on the border.

Superjoint Ritual's Mr. Joe Fazzio. American Racing Wheels' Mr. Steve "Big Fish" Zieber, the Panama Marlin King. And the good-groove road folks, Mr. Pablo "TourTime" Gamboa, D. Stuart, and Ms. Wendy Graham. And, of course, Mr. Pete Chapouris, Tony Thacker, and Jimmy Shine, along with their famed crew and hot-rod specialists at SO-CAL Speed Shop.

These are the movers and shakers and troublemakers that I love dearly. So check it out. I dig my pals and you'll dig these pages.

Luv,

Billy F Gibbons, 2005

THE COLLABORATORS

Born and raised in Boston, **Tom Vickers** moved to San Francisco in the early 1970s, where he was a writer for *Rolling Stone* and first saw ZZ Top on the Worldwide Texas Tour in 1975. He became friends with Mr. Gibbons in 1979 during the *Degüello* tour and has seen every ZZ Top tour since, remaining one of BFG's closest pals. A music-industry veteran, he is currently working on a number of DVD, book, and record projects. He lives in Los Angeles with his wife Victoria, son Alex, and faithful dog Cowboy.

Born in Denver and raised in Southern California, **David Perry** started burning film at age 10. He studied photography at Art Center College of Design in Pasadena, began his career as a professional photographer in 1986, and has since exhibited his work worldwide. His byline appears on three previous books, including *Hot Rod Pin-ups* (2004). Perry lives in Vallejo, California, plays rockabilly guitar, and in 1999 helped resurrect that city's Swanx car club. His work can be viewed at www.davidperrystudio.com.

PHOTOGRAPHY

All photography by David Perry, except: pages 14–19, 20 (top left and top right), 21 (right), 24–27, 30 (right), 31–43, 47–53, 57 (bottom left and top right), and 64–67, *Billy F Gibbons collection*; pages 72 (bottom) and 110 (top), *courtesy Tony Thacker/SO-CAL Speed Shop*; pages 124, 125 (top right), and 128, *Billy F Gibbons collection*; page 130, *courtesy Rick Gould*; page 131, *courtesy John Bolin*; pages 133 (center, center right, and bottom right), 148 (left), 152 (bottom right), 158 (center right), 173 (left), 175 (bottom right), and 177 (bottom left), *Billy F Gibbons collection*; page 190, top, *courtesy Jamie Chamberlin*; and page 192, *Billy F Gibbons collection*.

THE CARS

ELIMINATOR COUPE

Billy hooked up with Larry Wood for the design, and with Don Thelen at Buffalo Motor Cars for the actual build of this 1933 Ford, arguably the most recognizable hot rod on the planet. Wall Pantera fabricated the wheels and Kenny Youngblood painted the now-famous Z graphics on the sides of the red coupe. The Pete and Jake–fabricated chassis is mounted with a mill from Art Chrisman Engines, who outfitted it with an Edelbrock intake and Holly carbs.

LEAPIN' LIMO

Leapin' Limo began life as a 1948 Pontiac Silver Streak. It was built by Chuck Lombardo Sr. and Jr. at California Street Rods, who stretched in 40 inches and chopped it 4 ?. Powered by a Pontiac big block, Leapin' Limo rolls on American Racing wheels.

CADZZILLA

Billy and Larry Erickson, then a chief designer at GM, dreamed up this sleek 'n' sinister creation on a bar napkin in Mexico. Built in just six months in 1989 at Boyd Coddington's shop and based on a 1948 Cadillac Sedanette, the car roars with a 500-ci, 8.2-liter, fuel-injected Cadillac engine. The body, fabricated by Craig Naff, sits on hand-built rails and features a nosed hood, frenched headlights, and a '55 Chevy bumper with integrated guards. The rearview mirrors, fashioned from Cadillac bumper bullets, double as doorhandles, and the "Goddess" hood ornament is accommodated by a channel in the hood. The seamless hood and front fenders tilt forward, à la 1960s Gassers, and, like the fabricated disc hub caps and Moon tank set into the '49 Caddie grille, is more evocative of a hot rod than a custom. Almost exclusively hand-formed, the metal in the rear helps create a movement recalling Art Deco masters and the 1930s. The candy eggplant sprayed over gray changes color dramatically with the lighting, and its dark hues can easily be construed as a nod to the Harry Westergard style. Of all of CadZZilla's features, the license plate is one of the most prominent with its simple statement, 18 TOKYO.

HOGZZILLA

Conceived by Larry Erickson, HogZZilla 1 and 2 were based on 1991 Harley-Davidsons and built as escorts to Billy's famed CadZZilla. Pete Chapouris and Bob Bauer took care of fabrication at SO-CAL Speed Shop, customizing the Harley Fat Boys in 58 days.

MAMBO COUPE

The Mambo Coupe is based on a 1936 Ford three-window and was rodded at SO-CAL Speed Shop. It's powered by a 350 Chevy with Corvette headers and LT1 valve covers, and it breathes through a single Carter 500-cfm carburetor and Cal Custom air cleaner. Also under the louvered hood are an Amp Tech alternator and an Edelbrock Toker manifold. Power is transferred to the polished Rear Wheels wrapped in B. F. Goodrich rubber via a TH350 transmission. Mambo's interior was done by Ron Mangus and Custom Auto Interiors, who covered Mazda seats with some worn leather taken from Pete Chapouris' father's couch. JB Donaldson provided the steering wheel, and Vintage Air keeps the car cool when the 300-watt Alpine stereo with 10 custom-covered speakers heats things up.

KOPPERHED

Often described as the shoebox that Ford should have made, Kopperhed was born in 1950 as a five-window business coupe. Forty-five years later, Pete Chapouris of PC3g gave it a facelift—Billy style. Though deceptively conservative at first glance, the extensive bodywork includes a top that was chopped 3 inches, doors lengthened 10 inches, and filled-in side windows to create a three-window. Chapouris retained classic original components like the un-frenched headlights, door handles, iconic grille and bullet nose, and rear-fender beads (though the latter required some modification). Billy and Chapouris jammed econo when dropping the Ford, opting for heated coils and a pair of lowering blocks. Powered by a 312-ci 1957 Y-block Thunderbird Tri-Power with a three-pot Offy intake, Ford carbs, and re-pop air cleaner, all hooked up to a Ford three-speed with overdrive. Kopperhed slithers on 16-inch copper-colored wheels by PC3g wrapped with B. F. Goodrich rubber featuring removable whitewalls. Finned aluminum rocker covers sit above coated manifolds from a Ford F-600 pickup. Inside, Ron Mangus of Custom Auto Interiors did the white and copper-colored Tijuana-style tuck 'n' roll (the 20-year-old copper-colored leather was found in Oregon), while JB Donaldson restored the Crest Liner steering wheel. All of the instruments are original, though PC3g slightly modified the dash to accommodate the stereo.

SLAMPALA

One of Billy's daily drivers, this 1962 Impala was built in 1997 and 1998 at SO-CAL Speed Shop and California Street Rods. The power plant is a 1967 327 small block with a Bitchin Products re-pop Caddie air cleaner and chromed valve covers. Floating on a solenoid-controlled Firestone Air Ride Tech suspension system installed at SO-CAL, Slampala features pearlescent vinyl interior and a two-tone crème and mint green steering wheel and dash by JB Donaldson. Billy retained the original radio but had a CD player installed in the glovebox. And though the Madonna statue or mojo bag may steal your attention, nothing snags your eye more than Slampala's shoes. In the past, Slampala has been outfitted with 18- and 20-inch American Racing Hopsters and Racing Torq Thrust IIs; on these pages, it's shown with Mooneyes Spiders on 14-inch steelies wrapped in pinner whitewalls.

325I CUSTOM

Billy's Beemer could be described as a mild custom with just enough accoutrements to appease both the rockabilly and hip-hop sets. The 1992 model-year 325i sports a fully stamped 'n' louvered hot rod hood, as well as 8-ball logos to replace all of the BMW roundels on the trunk, hood, and wheels, not to mention an actual 8-ball on the shifter. For the Euro-car and billet enthusiasts, 8 Ball B rolls on four AZEV Type B wheels (sans center caps) from Germany.

CADILLAC '61

Billy acquired this 1961 Cadillac Coupe in 2004. He bought the basically stock machine from Tolle Road Customs in Mt. Vernon, Illinois, which had purchased the car from Air Ride Technologies in 2003. Basically stock, the Caddie does have an Air Ride system, as well as A/C installed by the fellas at Tolle Road.

'32 FORD HIGHBOY

Rudy Rodriguez of Fullerton Fabrications rodded this 1932 Ford highboy with a French-built V-8 flathead. A thoroughly classic hot rod right down to the 1939 banjo steering wheel and the Ford bullnose atop its grille shell, the roadster also features Sharp heads, dropped and drilled front axle, dual carbs topped by helmet air cleaners, a LaSalle tranny, Mercury hubcaps, and an engine-turned SO-CAL Speed Shop instrument panel.

INDEX

¿QUIEN ES ESTE HOMBRE?

A CONTIÑUACION...

visit www.billyfgibbons.com

BRASWELL MEMORIAL LIB

5401 9100 239 969 9
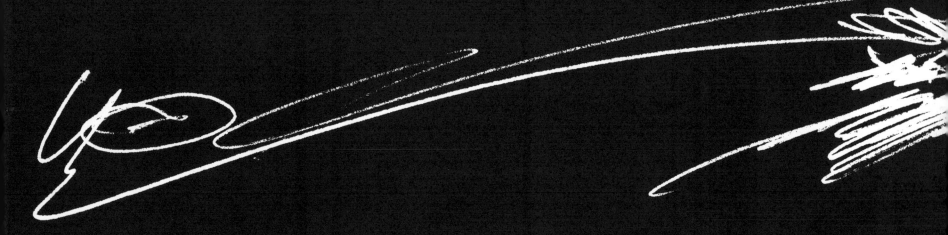